The Art Of HAPPINESS

HOW TO MANIFEST SUCCESS & ABUNDANCE IN 10 LESSONS

A 21 day Course in the 10 Formulas of Manifesting

Michael Rinne

ISBN: 0692682384

ISBN 13: 9780692682388

Book I

Book II

Foreword

Manifesting = Intent + Vision + Non-Resistance

I still remember the day when I came home from work. I had another day of stress and anxiety. I laid down on top of my bed. I could no longer deal with all the anxiety and fear in me. I wanted to give up. I could no longer live like this.

After a few years of great success my law firm suddenly experienced a fast downturn. There were no more new clients. The market had dried up. This shift came so suddenly that it hit me by surprise. I had to lay off all my employees and handle hundreds of legal cases by myself. The phone did not stop ringing. Angry clients calling about when their case would be completed while I was I struggling to pay my bills. There was no more income but thousands of monthly expenses. It was too much to handle.

This day when I was laying on top of my bed I was ready to give up. There was nothing I could do to save my firm or my marriage. It was all out of my hands.

I used to be a go getter. I have two law degrees, immigrated to America, built a thriving business and only the sky was the limit. None of this was valid anymore.

After about 20 minutes laying on top of my bed I had a profound experience that would change my life forever. I felt as if I was sucked out through the top of my head. Some force was spinning and pulling me out. I was about to leave my body. The spinning accelerated. I felt fear. I felt I was about to die. Suddenly the spinning stopped. I entered into a vast black space. I was floating in a vast universe. I felt utter peace.

All my anxiety was gone. I was detached from my body and from my life. After a few seconds I felt my body laying on the bed again. I got up. I felt streams of happiness and vitality enter my body. I jumped off the bed and danced through my house, smiling and laughing. All of this took place in a matter of half an hour.

From that day on my life changed forever. Despite my business collapsing and my marriage breaking apart I felt that I had entered a process of detachment. It was as if I lost the capacity to worry about all the things I used to worry about.

Now that I stopped worrying I had much more energy to handle the day to day business and I found time and money to get away from my law firm to continue my inner transformation. In the coming years incredible things have happened to me.

While my transformation is an ongoing process I have changed tremendously in the past three years. My once difficult relationship with my ex-wife has improved wonderfully. New business is coming in effortlessly and I am starting a new career to help people discover their inner creative powers.

I have been practicing mediation since I was twelve year old. I have done many spiritual retreats and visited spiritual gurus in India since I was a child. Awareness and consciousness are the cornerstones in life.

However only after my recent crisis in my life has the spiritual side in me taken the front seat. Now all the insights and experiences I have had over the course of my life are forming one coherent body of spiritual knowing. The insights from this knowing have found their way into this book.

I never thought I could write a book. I am following the call that I hear when I am still. There is no unbearable stress or anxiety in my new life. I feel like I am no longer alone doing all the work. The work itself is unfolding whenever I let go and surrender to what is happening at the moment.

We all suffer. Our suffering is inflicted by our hyper active and dysfunctional minds. We do not know how to become free and enjoy the beauty of life. We suffer from stress, anxiety, fear and a lack of purpose in life.

I wrote this book to help you find your way to manifest a life of happiness, success and abundance.

I want you to embrace your inner creative powers to manifest a life of joy, peace and success. I want you to experience the powers that are inside of you. The exercises in this book will help you on your path.

The book is based on my 21 day Manifestation Course. After three weeks of practicing the exercises you will be able to break free from what has kept you from enjoying your life. You will be able to manifest happiness, success and abundance.

Nothing in this book should be believed. Everything has to be experienced. There is no dogma and no teaching in this book. The book intends to provide you with the know-how for self-discovery and self-empowerment.

This book was written during an eight weeks stay in India.

Before I started writing the book I had no idea what I could write about. All I knew was I wanted to help people find lasting happiness and success. What ensued during those eight weeks in India was a constant flow of insights.

The insights and the exercises came to me after each morning and each evening meditation. Just like clock work the next chapter unfolded itself once the previous chapter was completed.

All of the exercises came to me in my meditations. Before I put them into this book, I practiced them on myself.

Everything in this book comes directly from my own experiences and insights.

The book is non-denominational and is based solely on my experiences. The purpose of this book is to inspire you to have your own experiences. Only what we experience ourselves is useful for us.

You too have the ability to receive the answers to your life's questions. When you are aware and non-resistant to the present moment, the answers will come to you. The book will empower you to accomplish this.

Introduction

The book is full of insights and practices to develop the powers you need, to create the life of happiness, success and wealth.

In the next 21 days you will master the 10 formulas of manifesting.

I recommend to use the full 21 days. Each chapter is followed by an exercise. Over the course of the next 21 days you will gain the required experiences to master and apply the 10 formulas.

The layout of the book into Book One and a Book Two is based on my insight that we first have to deconstruct the obstacles in our lives and lay a foundation before we can manifest our new life.

In order to manifest the life we want, we need to free ourselves from everything that keeps us from living our envisioned reality. Book One is designed to get you to the ground zero of your life. In Book Two you will be introduced to the concrete techniques and formulas of manifesting.

I developed and tested the exercises on myself. I am sharing my own experiences to illustrate how the spiritual principles can be experienced. Do not attempt to have the same experience. Every person's experience is different.

The exercises can be done once or several times. Once you completed all the exercises you can repeat them in any order.

To get the maximum benefit from this book I recommend to only proceed to Book Two after you have a thorough grip of the concepts of Book One.

Book One focuses on deconstructing everything that keeps us in a state of suffering and powerlessness. Unconsciousness and ignorance of our potential is form of suffering.

The terms used in this book grew out of my experiences. There is no need to put too much meaning into their linguistic definitions. The focus of this book is for you to gain your own experiences and it is not to teach a particular school of thought. The purpose of this book is to inspire you to start your journey into discovering your own truth.

In Book Two you will be introduced to the techniques of manifesting. Intent and Visualization are the guiding principles throughout Book Two.

Our physical health is crucial for our success. The less our emotional and mental states are distracted by our physical ailments the more energy we can dedicate to our transformation.

To support our body we should eat healthy and light and do physical exercise. In my experience when I exercise and eat a balanced diet I accomplish more on my spiritual path.

Our feelings and emotions affect our physical health. The same is true for our physical health. It affects our feelings, emotions and our spiritual states. Therefore by taking care of our body we are laying the foundation for emotional and spiritual growth. This does not mean that a healthy body is indispensible for spiritual growth, however if we have the choice we should improve our physical health for the sake of our emotional and spiritual well being.

Do the exercises when you feel awake, alert and when you are free from distraction. If however you have health problems do not let it prevent you from doing the exercises.

Even though the timing and length of the exercises are fixed, a person with health issues can adjust their duration. You can do the exercises at home or at work. Make sure that you are in a quiet place were you can practice for 21 minutes without disruption.

It may take more than one reading of this book to accomplish its goal. I certainly had to practice the exercises multiple times before I obtained measurable and lasting results.

Discover Your Manifesting Powers

Introduction

The wisdom of manifestation comes from deep inside of us. We must dig it out from under all the rubble that has accumulated throughout our lifetimes and beyond. Because of our mind driven consciousness the manifesting powers are hidden and inaccessible to most of us.

We are guided by our subconscious mental patterns. Some of them are beneficial but many are not. They hold us in a persistent state of suffering, fear, anxiety and wanting.

The book will help you to deconstruct these patterns and free your inert wisdom and creative powers.

Most problems in our lives are caused by our mind that has taken over our entire Self. It does not allow any space for all aspects of our Self to unfold.

The techniques in this book are designed to allow your mind to withdraw to its natural state, so that it can be used by your consciousness as a tool rather than being the cause of the problem. The techniques are holistic. They aim at empowering all the aspects of our Self to work together.

The simple act of relaxing the mind, letting it rest and withdraw has a tremendous impact on our quality of life.

Our mind resists whatever is happening at the present moment. Even positive experiences are resisted by the mind because it wants more of the positive experience. This prevents us from fully experiencing ourselves in the present moment. Because our mind insists on being in control of how we experience and how we perceive, we are prevented from enjoying the free flow of the experience. As a consequence we miss out on the possibility of enjoying a more wholesome perception of the experience.

The mind is not bad in itself. In fact it is highly efficient when used wisely. Today however most people's minds are dysfunctional and become victims of their minds.

The mind for the purpose of this book includes also our emotions. Emotions are our sensory feelings and perceptions after the mind has interpreted them based on its repertoire of pre-existing patterns. Our mind does not always interpret our perceptions and feelings to our greatest benefit. Our mind is driven by our limited subconscious patterns. Our patterns were caused by our experiences. Until we recognize our patterns and de-charge them, our mind will not function properly. It's entire modus operandi is based on these patterns. We must engage our awareness and consciousness to become free from our dysfunctional mind and allow it to become our tool.

The first step is to acknowledge the effect our mind has on us. In order to break free from its negative influence we have to get to ground zero. We must become aware of our suffering.

Most of our suffering and fear is not conscious. It is part of our subconscious. It is like a numb fear in us. When it becomes acute we feel it as fear. Once we feel it we can deal with it.

First we must become aware of our subconscious fear. We have grown accustomed to this undercurrent of fear that we only notice its existence after it has left us and we feel full of joy and happiness and we realize what we have missed out on all this time.

Our subconscious mind is not a bad per se. Along with our awareness it is the bridge to our higher consciousness.

The root of suffering is ignorance of our true nature. We do not know who we are and what we are capable of.

The first book is dedicated to deconstructing what is holding us back and the second book provides the tools to construct the life we want to have.

The book is organized according to the principle of active and passive. In spiritual practice as in life, being passive is just as important as being active. If we master the dance of active and passive, doing and letting go, intending and surrendering, we will reach our full potential.

Freedom from Suffering
My Story

Since I was a child I had fear of not having sufficient money to survive. I started saving money and accumulated a fair amount of it. Contrary to my inner fear I always had enough money. I became a successful lawyer and built a thriving law firm. Despite all the money however I could not enjoy my success. I feared I would lose all the money at any time. My fear culminated when my law firm began to lose business.

The marked had suddenly turned. I had to lay off all my employees. My case load grew exponentially. I was overwhelmed by stress and fear. I was struggling to pay the company bills. Weather I was at work or at home I was in constant stress and fear of survival. The market had completely disappeared and there was little I could do to rescue my firm. I lost my savings and my livelihood.

One day I came home from another stressful day at work. I laid down and just wanted to give up, not think anything, just be and surrender.

I was tired of fighting and expecting, wishing and wanting. I just wanted to be whatever I was at the moment.

I completely gave up. The pressure of the circumstances became too overwhelming. I began to accept whatever happened to me.

Strangely in the middle of utter despair I felt deep inner peace emerge. I felt freedom rise up from inside of me. This feeling transformed into optimism and vitality. I jumped off the bed and walked around my house. Suddenly I was full of energy. Gone was the feeling of lethargy.

I felt enthusiastic and empowered to embark onto a new phase in my life. My dire situation now felt like a blessing. My suffering had set me free to do something new, something that would nurture and empower me and help me find happiness and freedom.

This experience did not lead to a permanent detachment from all suffering. However it made me realize that there is a simple path to freedom. I realized that we already have all the powers to create a life of happiness, success and abundance inside of us.

My wife and friends were puzzled by how I handled the crash of my business. The worse the financial situation got the better I felt. I was on the path of detachment. I could see the light at the end of the tunnel. I experienced that joy and inner peace are not the result of my external accomplishments but rather my natural state of being. I began to feel safe and secure from inside.

Later I realized this fear was one of my mental patterns. This pattern had been deeply ingrained in my subconscious. My drive for financial security prevented me from recognizing the opportunities that were right in front of me. My mind was too occupied with its fear of survival. I could only see my situation through my fear colored lenses. I perceived my financial situation worse than it really was.

When my external difficulties became too intense to bear I surrendered. I began to acknowledge my fear as what it was, without fighting or judging it.

By detaching from my fear there was no more energy feeding it. Even though I had less money I could better enjoy the money I had. Strangely I felt more wealthy now. I still had the desire to be financially secure and successful but my desire was not motivated by fear but by the joy these circumstances bring.

The Freedom Formula
Introduction

To manifest what we want, we must identify the forces that prevent us from enjoying our lives. There are no inherently bad or negative energies, feelings or forces. Negative in this sense is our ignorance of our powers which has created an imbalance between the different aspects of our Self.

Our bodies want one thing while our minds want another thing. This imbalance prevents us from breaking through the cycle of fear and desire. We constantly want to escape one thing and acquire another. In this madness we hurt ourselves and others.

Suffering is manifested not only as an acute feeling but rather as a dull state of consciousness. We may feel that life is ok but it is not wonderful.

After we have awakened to our inner freedom, our ordinary limited state of unconsciousness is being felt more acutely than for a person who has not yet taken the step to awaken. For the unconscious person it is usually external circumstances that create discomfort and suffering where for the person who is on the path to awaken it is the knowing that there is a better life waiting but it has not yet fully materialized.

There is hardly any time in the day to simply *be* and feel alive. When we finally catch some time, we do not know how to quiet down our mind.

We use our minds to make ourselves feel good, which provides only temporary relief.

Our mind interprets everything we experience with our senses. It is controlled by our individual mental patterns. Our mental patterns have been formed by our past experiences. Because our mind is limited in its interpretation of our perception by our individual subconscious patterns it can only change its interpretation when our patterns change. Our patterns only change with the help of new powerful experiences. This dependency on our past experiences renders our mind utterly limited. Our limited mind may be enough for us to survive and get by, however it is not enough to fully enjoy our lives and become the masters of our destiny.

To determine our destiny we must free our limited perception. We must go beyond the boundaries of our known Self. When we have widened our span of perception we will perceive angles of reality that will allow us to become free.

In the state of deep mental and physical relaxation we reach a state of equilibrium. Our inherent wisdom and creative powers begin to emerge.

At this state, our mind will be clear and focused. It will function with less thoughts. In deep relaxation we reduce the mental pressure on our bodies and on our consciousness. As a consequence our consciousness begins to unfold, strengthen and to take the lead in our lives.

First we must relax our bodies, feelings, emotions and thoughts. We must give up our ambitions and expectations. Everything has to slow down.

Deep relaxation opens our body on all levels. Through these openings we will sink deeper and deeper into ourselves and uncover our inherent natural states of love, joy and inner peace. Our feelings begin to flow.

Our sensory perceptions become clear and crisp. We receive intuitive insights. These insights come from our consciousness. In this state we transform our subconscious patterns of which fear, anxiety and wanting are the most pervasive ones.

Instead of fighting or ignoring our suffering we must learn to locate it in our body and identify its meaning. Our suffering cannot be transformed with willpower alone. The tool to accomplish this is our sensory feeling. Through non-resistance to whatever we feel we become free from it. Through awareness we recognize the meaning of our suffering as it holds the key to our happiness.

Instead of vilifying our negative emotions, we must not resist them. We should not deny their existence. And if we cannot help but suppress our negative feelings then we must practice non-resistance to our inability to be non-resistant. Eventually we reach a point where we are non-resistant.

The Freedom Formula

Formula I : <u>Suffering – Dysfunctional Mind = Freedom</u>

*When we remove the dysfunction from our mind we
become free*

We all have physical, mental, emotional and spiritual suffering. In this chapter we will focus on our mental and emotional suffering. Emotional suffering belongs to the same category as mental suffering. Emotions being mind interpreted sensory feelings are part of the mind. Examples of emotions are fear, anger, hatred, anxiety, stress, wanting, craving, jealously, envy and others. All conditional emotions ultimately cause suffering. Even happiness, ultimately causes suffering.

Feelings are causeless and unconditional. They do not need a reason to exist. Feelings are joy, love, compassion and inner peace. These distinctions between emotions and feels are only meaningful in the context of this book.

The term "negative emotion" is used to distinguish it from enjoyable and pleasant emotions. Negative is not to be understood in a moral sense. They are not bad or useless. To the contrary they are often gateways to higher consciousness.

Unnecessary, mind created fear is a part of our daily lives. We make money out of fear, we keep jobs we don't like and we have relationships that do not nurture us. We are holding on to many unhealthy circumstances out of fear.

We are caught in a net of mind created fear and subconscious patterns, which prevent us from experiencing and perceiving life with its many opportunities. Our life energy is drained by our attempts to break free from suffering. We are caught in constant resistance to what is. Unfortunately we use our mind to become free from it. This never works. We deny our fear, play it down, force a positive perspective on our minds, or suppress it until we feel numb and forget about it. However until we identify our fear and allow us to feel it fully with our senses, we cannot experience the full power of love, joy and inner peace that are buried underneath our fear.

Fear has its place. It is needed and it serves a purpose. The fear however which causes all our problems is our mind created fear and our mental reaction to our physical feeling of fear.

Our fear is reflected in our physical bodies. Sometimes we are not aware of our fear and have no physical reaction to it. Often anxiety and stress are felt physically in our belly area and in our shoulders. We get ulcers from stress. We get migraine from being overwhelmed. To free ourselves from this fear instead of analyzing our symptoms we must feel the fear at its impact area which is our physical bodies.

Once we direct our awareness onto our body we must locate the area where the feeling of fear is located. In deep relaxation our mind will quiet down and our sensory perception of the fear sharpens.

In the context of this book I refer to "feeling" as being a sensory perception such as hearing, seeing, tasting, smelling and tactile feeling.

Fear of survival has been part of our pattern for thousands of years. All feelings are already dormant inside of us. Our reaction to external circumstances triggers the feelings to become active.

When we locate an emotion with our awareness in our body and recognize the underlying sensory feeling that is associated with it, we allow our emotion to become detached from our mind. When our emotion becomes detached from the mind it loses its particular mental label and can be felt in our body as a sensation. Our awareness can then focus on the feeling as a sensory experience without mental involvement. At this step we are able to deal with the sensation without the interference of our mind.

The next step is to stay with the sensation. The key is not to resist the feeling but to let it unfold. The feeling may grow stronger at first. It may move into a different area of our body or it may become subtle and expand throughout our body and eventually dissipate. All of these processes should be experienced without judgment and without any expectation.

Our focused awareness on our feelings causes the feelings to lose their density. The feelings begin to move. Once they move we experience a shift in our feelings.

Our body has its own intelligence and knows how to deal with its feelings. In order for our body to focus its resources on transforming our negative feelings, it needs the help of our focused awareness. Therefore we must grow our awareness. Our focused awareness on our feelings exposes the feelings into the light where we can see them and deal with them.

In the absence of awareness our fear remains stuck in our minds and is being reflected by our bodies. We feel it as a dense unpleasant and painful blockage. Mostly we do not recognize our blockages for what they are but experience them as physical discomfort and illness. Dense energy does not move. It is like a blanket covering our inherent positive feelings underneath. These blockages make us physically, emotionally and mentally sick.

When our feelings begin to move, we experience an opening in our body. Through this opening our inherent positive feelings emerge.

We do not need to eradicate all our blockages and negative emotions. It is enough to be aware of them. Some unpleasant feelings may never fully disappear. However we no longer suffer from these feelings once we recognize their purpose for us.

In my own experience I realized that my fear of not having enough money was located in my belly area. I feel it as a tight knot. By not resisting to it and not resisting to my resistance, the knot loosens, moves and eventually dissipates. I can still feel the fear in the space around me, however now I experience it as an impersonal fear which does not belong to me any longer. I become detached from it. The space in my body that was once occupied by this fear is now filled with joy.

Fear can motivate people to achieve great things in life. Many people have became wealthy because they wanted to escape their fear of poverty. However a fear based life will always be fear based even after we have acquired external security and wealth. Fear will remain a part of us and prevent us from fully enjoying our lives.

Therefore the starting point to a happy and successful life is right where we are at this moment. We must become aware of our suffering and our fear and deal with it before we focus on manifesting a better life. The transformation of our fear releases energy that we will use to manifest.

We have to start from where we are in order to get to where we want to go. To manifest what we want we have to use our resources that lay dormant beneath the suffering and fear.

The formula to detach from suffering is:

Suffering – Dysfunctional Mind = Freedom

When we have freed ourselves from our dysfunctional mind, what is left is a functional mind. We will free ourselves by untangling our mind from its dependency on our obsolete subconscious patterns.

When we have freed ourselves from our fear based subconscious patterns we will perceive ourselves and the world in a new light. Our perception will now perceive reality from a wider angle. As we change internally so will the external circumstances. The external world will flourish and prosper as will our inner feelings.

Surrendering into Freedom

When our bodies and minds are fully relaxed, our dysfunctional mind patterns begin to lose their grip on us and we undergo a transformation.

In the state of relaxation we are able to sense the feelings that are in our body. When we fully focus our awareness on the feeling, our mind has nothing to be occupied with. So it withdraws. In this relaxed state, our inherent feelings of peace, love and joy emerge.

Deep relaxation is different from sleeping, daydreaming or dozing. In deep relaxation we are highly alert and our mind is sharp.

Deep relaxation consists of active as well as passive components. The active components are non-resistance and gratitude. These states are being initiated with our intent. After we have formed the intent to relax we must relax into non-resistance and gratitude and experience these states passively. At this point we ride the wave of the experience. This is the passive component.

Once our physical body is relaxed, our mind will eventually relax as well and withdraw into the background. Now when we direct our awareness onto our feelings in our body we strengthen our awareness. Step by step our awareness moves into the foreground and it becomes our guide in our lives.

When we are non-resistant to whatever we feel and perceive, we allow ourselves to sink deeper into ourselves. We should not expect any particular outcome nor attempt to force a relaxed state on us. Anything we attempt with our mind will cause our subconscious mind to cause the opposite of what we want to be manifested.

To illustrate how our subconscious mind works, imagine you are attempting to become relaxed by using your mind. With your will power you push yourself to be relaxed. This causes your subconscious to tell you that because you are trying to be relaxed, you are not relaxed yet. In other words whenever we desire something and we hold on to our desire we send out the signal to our subconscious that we are lacking the very thing we desire. Without being conscious of it we create the opposite of what we want.

The key to attaining deep relaxation is to give up the wanting for it. After we have formed the initial intentional impulse to relax we have to give up our expectation to get there. We have to ride the waves of our feelings without holding on to them. We must not attempt to manipulate, enhance or suppress what we experience.

If we cannot become non-resistant to whatever is, we must accept this and become non-resistant to being resistant. This in itself is non-resistance.

The second intentional impulse to gain deep relaxation is gratitude. Gratitude has the function to acknowledge the reality of whatever is at the present moment. It prevents our mind to hold on, change, enhance or deny whatever is. Gratitude causes us to be present. Gratitude completes whatever experience we have and thus enables us to move on to the next experience. When we experience gratitude we send out the signal to our subconscious that our experience is real and thus our subconscious has no reason to create the reality of lack of the very experience we just had.

For example if we desire to be deeply relaxed, when we reach that state, until we express gratitude, our initial desire to be relaxed will carry on and thus causing our subconscious to believe that we are not relaxed. Gratitude signals to our subconscious that we have obtained what we desired and as such it releases our subconscious from having to cause its opposite into reality.

By expressing gratitude we also acknowledge that our efforts have succeeded. This acknowledgment creates a new pathway which will make future efforts more easy. This new pathway is a new positive pattern in ourselves, which will make it easier for us to reach the same state the next time we do the exercise. Continuous practice opens the pathways requiring less and less energy to reach the desired state.

Feelings vs. Emotions

The most effective tool to reach liberation from our dysfunctional mind is our sensory feelings. Our sensory feelings are the carrier on which our awareness rides. Awareness rests on our feelings and rides it to reach more and more subtle states of consciousness to a point where there are no more feelings and all that is left is consciousness.

For the purpose of this book feelings are defined as sensory perceptions. Examples are: feeling cold, warm, movement, fast, slow, opening, expansion, gross or subtle. Into this category we also include feelings of love, joy and inner peace. Feelings are absolute as opposed to relative. In other words the feeling of cold for example exists in its own right without requiring mental reasoning.

Emotions on the other hand are composed of sensory feelings with a mental component. When we feel with our senses, our mind interprets the feeling with the help of its repertoire of past experiences and mental patterns. The interpreted sensory feeling is defined in this book as an emotion. Emotions include, happy, sad, angry, jealous, satisfied, content, wanting, craving etc. Emotions are relative because they depend on each person's individual mental interpretation and perception.

To illustrate how the mind is involved in our emotions think about the conditional nature of our emotions. For example we are sad because of our individual perception of a certain circumstance or we are happy because in our perception a particular circumstance is beneficial to us. On the other hand while feelings also exist because of particular circumstances (i.e. we are cold because it is cold outside), they are detached from our perception and from our inner patterns and as such are free from our mind. It is possible to experience a sensory feeling without any thought. Because feelings are not born in our mind but rather free standing, and independent of the mind, we use feelings rather than emotions to free us from the mind.

Before a person has interpreted the feeling it is neutral. It is free from judgment. It is neither good nor bad. It is independent of our personal limited perception.

It is not that emotions are not helpful in spiritual practice. To the contrary they are door openers to access our sensory feelings. For example through the emotion of sadness we gain access to our sensory feeling of sadness in our body.

As long as we feel our emotions without hanging on to the story about them, we will accomplish the same result.

Emotions as opposed to feelings cause us to see reality through our limited individual mental filter. Emotions are part of our mind and just like thoughts they filter the reality as we perceive it and prevent us from experiencing the true essence of what we perceive. Only after we have removed our mental filter can we see the true essence of what we perceive. Only the person who can truly see the reality as it is, will understand its essence and can fully enjoy it. This is a necessary prerequisite for manifesting ones own reality.

Feelings have different states of consistency. For example a feeling can be felt as physical. In that consistency the feeling is easily located in our physical body. For example stress can often be felt in our guts. A feeling can be more subtle as well. It can be so subtle that we would not think of it as a feeling but rather relate to it as an experience. For example love can be felt very physically as a warm sensation in our general heart area. However once this feeling expands it becomes more and more subtle to a point where we do not physically feel it but rather experience it.

Love in its very subtle state can be experienced as an atmosphere that fills the space around us. Apart from our physical body we have several subtle bodies. Feelings in our subtle bodies are still feelings however we experience them rather than physically sensing them. When our feelings expand even further they transform into states of consciousness. States of consciousness are known rather than experienced.

The higher our feelings travel and the subtler they become, the more we learn about their true essence. For example the feeling of love is first experienced as a warm pleasant sensation. When it expands and reaches our subtle body it transforms into compassion. In its most subtle state it can be described as a state of consciousness. At this state it is beyond the realm of experience.

Feelings transform into wisdom in their most subtle form.

In this book we will learn to ride our feelings step by step through the levels of our bodies high up into pure consciousness.

Freedom from our limited Perception

In order to become free from suffering we must free our perception from its limitations.

To free our perception we apply the following steps.

Once we have located the particular feeling in our body that is connected to our suffering, we must become aware of the fact that the suffering is caused by our perception of it.

We must shine the light of our awareness onto our perception of the feeling that is connected with our suffering. With the help of our awareness we become aware of our perception. This process frees our perception from its rigid limited focus. Our perception begins to shift, change and transform into a new perception while the object of our perception remains unchanged. In other words we will see what we have seen all along in a new light.

We cannot free our perception from our mind by using our mind. However when we are aware of our perception and accept and do not resist, our perception will cease to be rigid. It becomes fluid. In its fluid state, our perception has the agility to shift and take on new viewpoints of reality. When our perception is free it will show a wider and more wholesome picture of reality. Our perception begins to reveal angles of reality that we have missed before. By practicing gratitude we allow our inherent positive feelings to emerge that will guide our perception to take on a viewpoint that will mirror our new inner positive state.

This is not about creating an artificial perception with our mind. This has nothing to do with positive thinking. To the contrary, it is about perceiving what is really in front of us. In being aware of our perception as it perceives reality, our perception opens up on its own.

Our perception is only able to perceive those aspects of reality that our mind is familiar with and that our mind is able to interpret. This is because we only have a limited repertoire of experiences and patterns that serve as a reference against which our perception functions.

Before we experience anything in this world, our perception has already altered whatever we perceive. Our perception alters what we perceive into a reality that fits our pre-existing inner patterns, which in turn have been formed by our past experiences. Since we only have a limited repertoire of experiences and patterns, we cannot perceive large aspects of reality. Therefore we only know very little about the things we perceive. May that be external or internal realities.

To illustrate how limited and relative our perception is consider the following example:

> A person who has only a small salary may perceive a $20,000 credit card debt as an insurmountable burden and as a result feel tremendous anxiety. This person may not even be aware of the fact that it is his or her perception which is causing the anxiety and not the debt itself. There is no anxiety inherent in credit card debt. Imagine a person who has the same credit card

debt but makes $500,000.00 a year. This person would probably not experience the same anxiety. To take this example one step further, even if both people have the same income, they would likely have different percep- tions of their $20,000 credit card debt. A pessimistic person may suffer from fear while an optimistic person may see an opportunity in it. The reason we perceive the same reality in drastically different ways is rooted in our individual subconscious patterns that shape our perception.

All external realities are relative and temporary. In our example: A $20,000.00 credit card debt is nothing more than debt. It is not a large debt nor a small debt, neither a difficult debt to deal with nor an easy debt to wipe out. The quality of the external reality depends only on the perception of the observer.

External circumstances come and go. Our patterns are there to stay. Life has ups and downs but our fear is constant. It is either dormant or acute.

Just as all external reality is temporary and relative to the perceiver so are our feelings. As long as our feelings are perceived and interpreted by our limited mind, we are not able to see their absolute and permanent essence.

Our perception must detach from the mind and find a new absolute reference point from which to perceive.

Therefore when we open ourselves with the help of non-resistance and gratitude, our perception can find permanent ground to anchor itself in. The more we find our true essence, the more our perception will perceive the essence of everything it perceives. The essence of all things is permanent and absolute. It does not relate to anything because it is one with everything.

There is nothing inherently wrong with our limited perception as long as we are aware of its limitations. Seeing is knowing and knowledge empowers us to change.

Through detachment and deep relaxation we begin to understand that our perception of reality is not the only possible perception. We become aware of the temporary and fluid nature of our perception.

Detachment from our limited perception frees us from suffering. When we are free from suffering our inherent creative powers emerge. When we have detached our perception from our limited mind we are able to decide how we want to perceive. We begin to control our perception instead of being controlled by it. This process is required to be able to perceive reality in its entirety. Only when we are able to perceive reality in its entirety will we be able to focus on those aspects of reality that are beneficial to us.

Our perception mirrors whatever state of consciousness we are in.

Once our perception has been free from our limited mind and has been successfully anchored in our true and absolute essence it begins to naturally gravitate towards aspects and viewpoints of reality that mirror our true essence. Our true essence is free from destructive and detrimental tendencies. When our perception has been cleared from all negative aspects it will lead us to joy, inner peace and love which is what we need in order to be able to manifest.

Freedom from Future and Past

Future and the past are mental concepts and when we relate to them as such they only exist in our minds. For our mind however they are solid reality and deeply affect our lives.

As long as we hold on to the future and the past as concepts and perceive them as reality we suffer. Our suffering is caused by our feeling of powerlessness. We are powerless because we have no control over the future and the past. Neither of the two can be experienced nor changed.

We worry about the future. However there is nothing we can do about the future at the present moment. When we worry about the future our subconscious concludes that we worry about something that does not yet exist. How can we resolve something that does not yet exist ? This feeling of powerlessness causes anxiety and stress.

The same is true for the concept of the past. When we dwell in the past we re-experience past events and feelings. Since these events and feelings are no longer in existence we cannot do anything about them.

The key to break the suffering is to realize that while events and feelings are real, the idea of them as being in the past or future is an illusion of the mind.

When we worry about the future or suffer from our past, the one thing that is real is the worry we have at the present moment. We must become aware and focus on this feeling we have and decouple it from the concept of future or past. By practicing non-resistance to the feelings we have about the future or past, the feelings lose their power and will either transform or dissipate. As long as we are aware of the fact that the feeling about a future or past reality is currently existing in us, we have the power to deal with it in the present moment.

Even positive feelings about the future or past can have negative effects on our well-being. The reason is that when we think about a positive event or circumstance as happening in the future or the past our subconscious automatically causes us to experience its non-existence. The experience of its non-existence reduces the positive effect the particular feeling would otherwise have.

While we have to use the concepts of past and future in our daily lives, these concepts will stop affecting us negatively when we realize that we have power to determine how we feel about them at the present moment.

Day 1

Breathing Exercise

The exercises can be done at home, in your office, in the car or wherever you have a quiet spot and you are free from distractions.

The goal of this exercise is to relax your mind, to slow down your stream of thoughts and to access your feelings.

The result of the exercise will be that your mind withdraws, allowing love, joy and inner peace to arise.

The breathing exercise will calm your mind and prepare you for the other exercises in this book.

Do this exercise for 21 minutes.

Lay down or sit comfortably.

Close your eyes or leave them half way open whatever feels more comfortable.

Become aware of your breath. Do not actively focus on your breath. Be aware that there is breathing inside of you.

Breathe passively. Let the breathing happen and feel the air flowing through your body. Feel how your body is being touched by your breathing.

Allow your breath to become subtle.

Now become aware of yourself observing your breath. Be aware of your awareness.

Relax and sink deeper. Relax deeper and deeper.

After 21 minutes slowly open your eyes and express gratitude for how you feel now.

Deep Relaxation Exercise

The goal of this exercise is to reach a state of deep physical and mental relaxation.

In deep relaxation we become aware of our feelings and we lose identification with our mind.

Before you relax each body part, you will shift your awareness onto the body part to have maximum benefit.

This exercise will last 21 minutes. Make sure you are undisturbed for the next 21 minutes. Turn off your cell phone.

Lay down or sit comfortably.

Close your eyes or leave them half open whatever feels more comfortable.

Relax your body.
Be aware of your body.

Shift your awareness to your feet.
Relax your feet.

Shift your awareness to your lower legs.
Relax your lower legs.

Shift your awareness to your upper legs.
Relax your upper legs.

Shift your awareness to your hips.
Relax your hips.

Shift your awareness to your lower back
Relax your lower back.

Shift your awareness to your back
Relax your back.

Shift your awareness to your shoulders.
Relax your shoulders.

Shift your awareness to your neck.
Relax your neck.

Shift your awareness to your upper arm.
Relax your upper arm.

Shift your awareness to your lower arm.
Relax your lower arm.

Shift your awareness to your hands.
Relax your hands.

Shift your awareness to your belly.
Relax your belly.

Shift your awareness to your chest.
Relax your chest.

Shift your awareness to your throat.
Relax your throat.

Shift your awareness to your lips.
Relax your lips.

Shift your awareness to your nose.
Relax your nose.

Shift your awareness to your eyes
Relax your eyes.

Shift your awareness to your skull.
Relax your skull.

Shift your awareness to the top of your head.
Relax the top of your head.

Inhale deeply.
Hold your breath for 30 seconds then exhale and relax your entire body.

Again inhale deeply.
Hold your breath for 30 second then exhale and relax your entire body.

Feel your entire body being relaxed.

Feel gratitude for being relaxed. Enjoy the feeling of relaxation and the feeling of gratitude.

Sink deeper and deeper.

If you are sleepy that is fine. You can take a nap.

If you feel you cannot relax do not force yourself. Accept that you cannot relax. And if you cannot accept that you cannot relax do not worry, simply accept whatever is happening inside of you.

Be non-resistant to whatever you feel.

Do not expect any particular result from this exercise.

Sink deeper and enjoy your state. Nobody is judging you.

Relax deeper.

Open your eyes.
Look around the room. Notice any change in your perception. Get up slowly.

Conclude the exercise.

Freedom from Suffering Exercise

The goal of this exercise is to reach a state of deep relaxation. From this state we will loosen and soften our feelings of fear and suffering. This exercise will free us from the grip of these patterns.

Use a timer to time the intervals of the exercise.

The exercise is 21 minutes.

Breathing Exercise for seven minutes
Lay down or sit comfortably.

Close your eyes or leave them half way open whatever feels more comfortable.

Become aware of your breath. Do not actively focus on your breath. Be aware that there is breathing inside of you.

Breathe passively. Let the breathing happen and feel the air flowing through your body. Feel your body how it is being touched inside by your breathing.

Allow your breath to become subtle.

Now become aware of yourself observing your breath. Be aware of your awareness.

Relax and sink deeper. Relax deeper and deeper.

◆ ◆ ◆

Deep Relaxation Exercise for seven minutes
For seven minutes do the deep relaxation exercise.

Relax your body.
Be aware of your body.

Shift your awareness to your feet.
Relax your feet.

Shift your awareness to your lower legs.
Relax your lower legs.

Shift your awareness to your upper legs.
Relax your upper legs.

Shift your awareness to your hips.
Relax your hips.

Shift your awareness to your lower back.
Relax your lower back.

Shift your awareness to your back.
Relax your back.

Shift your awareness to your shoulders.
Relax your shoulders.

Shift your awareness to your neck.
Relax your neck.

Shift your awareness to your upper arm.
Relax your upper arm.

Shift your awareness to your lower arm.
Relax your lower arm.

Shift your awareness to your hands.
Relax your hands.

Shift your awareness to your belly.
Relax your belly.

Shift your awareness to your chest.
Relax your chest.

Shift your awareness to your throat.
Relax your throat.

Shift your awareness to your lips
Relax your lips.

Shift your awareness to your nose.
Relax your nose.

Shift your awareness to your eyes
Relax your eyes.

Shift your awareness to your skull.
Relax your skull.

Shift your awareness to the top of your head.
Relax the top of your head.

Inhale deeply.
Hold your breath for 30 seconds then exhale and relax your entire body.

Again inhale deeply.
Hold your breath for 30 seconds, then exhale and relax your entire body.

Feel your entire body relaxed.

Feel gratitude for being relaxed. Enjoy the feeling of relaxation and the feeling of gratitude.

Sink deeper and deeper.

If you are sleepy that is fine. You can take a nap.

If you feel you cannot relax do not force it. Accept that you cannot relax. And if you cannot accept that you cannot relax do not worry simply accept whatever is happening inside of you.

Be non-resistant to whatever you feel.

Do not expect any particular result from this exercise.

Sink deeper and enjoy your state. Nobody is judging you.

Relax deeper.

♦ ♦ ♦

Now focus on a feeling you are familiar with. For example anxiety about finances, problems in your relationship or any other unpleasant feeling.

Be aware of your entire body. Feel your body.

Now try to locate this particular feeling in our body.

For example I usually feel anxiety in my intestinal area.

When you have located the feeling stay with it and experience it with your senses.

If the feeling does not emerge or if it quickly subsides do not hold on to it. Do not enhance or elongate it either. Experience whatever is at the present moment.

Do not resist whatever you feel, let it be however it feels. If you have the urge to express your feeling verbally, do so.

Now that you have located the physical feeling of your suffering, all you have to do is stay with it and we aware of it.

If no feeling emerges or if you cannot locate the feeling in your body, feel how you feel about this. Stay with this feeling. If you believe you have no feeling whatsoever then accept this and be open to whatever you experience.

If thoughts and emotions emerge let them come. If you do not grasp them nor push them away they will come and go. Be non-resistant.

Be non-judgmental about what is happening at this moment. Let go of judging yourself.

Feel how the initially dense feeling of suffering moves and becomes more subtle once you put your awareness onto it.

Be grateful that you can be aware and feel your suffering inside your body without being incapacitated by it. You are becoming detached from it.

Feel your feeling of gratitude. What does it feel like ?

Be grateful for the feeling your gratitude gives you.

Conclude the exercise.

Freedom from Limited Perception Exercise

The goal of this exercise is to change your perception about your suffering in order to become free from it.

Use a timer to time the intervals of the exercise.

The exercise will be fourteen minutes.

Seven Minute Breathing Exercise
Lay down or sit comfortably.

Close your eyes or leave them half way open whatever feels more comfortable.

Become aware of your breath. Do not actively focus on your breath. Be aware that there is breathing inside of you.

Breathe passively. Let the breathing happen and feel the air flowing through your body. Feel your body how it is being touched inside by your breathing.

Allow your breath to become subtle.

Now become aware of yourself observing your breath. Be aware of your awareness.

Relax and sink deeper. Relax deeper and deeper.

♦ ♦ ♦

Now focus on a familiar feeling For example your anxiety about finances, issues in a relationship or any other unpleasant feeling.

Be aware of your body. Now Locate the feeling in our body. Is it in your belly area, in your chest or around your shoulders ?

Stay with the feeling. Experience it with your senses.

If the feeling does not fully emerge or if it quickly subsides do not try to hold on to it. Do not enhance or elongate it. Experience whatever is at the present moment.

Do not resist the feeling. Let it be however it feels. If you have to express your feeling express it. However there is no need to express it.

You have activated your intention to locate and feel your suffering. From now on all that is required from you is to stay with whatever feeling arises.

If thoughts and emotions emerge let them come. Be non-resistant to them. If you do not grasp them or push them away, they will come and go.

Be non-judgmental to whatever happens. Let go of judging yourself. Do not have any expectation of what you want to happen. Your initial intent will carry you through the exercise.

Be aware of how the dense feeling of suffering begins to move and become subtle.

Be grateful that you are aware and that you feel your suffering inside your body without being incapacitated by it.

Be grateful for having gotten to this step.

Feel your gratitude.

◆ ◆ ◆

Now become aware of your perception of your feeling.

Do not judge, deny or enhance your perception. Simply we aware of the act of perceiving.

Notice any change in your feeling in your body now that you are aware of your perception of your feeling.

Experience your perception as if it was a feeling. As if it was tangible.

Notice if your perception begins to expand. If nothing happens that is perfectly fine. Do not resist whatever happens or whatever does not happen.

If you cannot give up resisting then give up your desire to not resist.

If your perception moves and expands, notice how that feels. You may feel a new emptiness inside of you. Notice if a different feeling emerges in the spot where the emptiness arose.

A new feeling may arise from your suffering. And a new perception may arise in you about the cause of your suffering. Be aware of it.

Feel the your gratitude.

Slowly open your eyes.

Complete the exercise.

The Powerful Mind Formula

Formula: <u>Dysfunctional Mind + Awareness + Consciousness = Powerful Mind</u>

Where the mind retreats consciousness emerges.

A large part of our day is occupied with repetitive thoughts and thoughts about thoughts. Our mind is overbearing and dysfunctional. We create mental stories about our thoughts. We judge ourselves and others. We judge ourselves for judging ourselves. Some thoughts we push away, some we try to suppress and others we crave and long for. We suffer from an overactive mind. We feel that we are limited by our mind. However we do not know how to escape from this condition.

Our mind consists of our thoughts, our subconscious and of our emotions.

We should not annihilate our mind however we need a more healthy and well functioning mind. We want a mind that is there when we need it. When it is not needed it should withdraw and be in a state of still alertness.

Our mind is an important part of our Self and when handled properly it is extremely powerful. Every exercise we do and every activity we start in our daily lives requires our intentional mental impulse. Even to relax from our minds we require a mental intention to do so. What we do not need however is a mind that does not let go; a mind that carries on and on.

There is nothing wrong with thoughts. Thoughts come and go. However our mind is tangled up in thoughts about thoughts and judgments about thoughts. It is a never ending cycle. This condition causes suffering. Our mind depletes our life energy. Carry-over thoughts are thoughts about thoughts and thoughts about thoughts about thoughts. They cause a vicious cycle of rehashing. We are trapped in a constant mental overstimulation. Because of this we are unable to feel alive and we cannot think and act intelligently.

Even more troubling than our over stimulated thoughts is our fear and suffering. Fear and suffering are rooted deeply in our subconscious patterns. These patterns are often latent and mostly we do not know about their existence. However they determine how we feel and act. When our fear and suffering is acute and we are aware of it we can address it and then change it. Therefore we must become aware of our subconscious patterns, bring them into the light of our awareness and allow them to transform.

In spiritual practice we attempt to reduce our thoughts. However by doing so we become overly judgmental about our thoughts and about ourselves. We attempt to quiet our minds with the tools of our mind. In reality we only shift our mental activity. What we really need is less mind and more consciousness.

The mind wants to linger in the future. We worry about the future. Because the future is a creation of the mind the mind prefers to linger in it. The only thing the mind can do about the future is either day dream or worry. This causes, delusion, stress and anxiety.

When we become detached from our mental activities, our suffering ends. There will always be mental activity such as thoughts and emotions, worry, anger and jealousy, however these mental symptoms begin to flow through us without affecting us deeply. We will not be free from fear but free with fear. All our mental symptoms will be there but they will no longer define who we are. Slowly through transformation our, mental activity will slow down.

Our minds should not unnecessarily linger in the future or in the past. It is harmless to enjoy memories of the past as long as we dwell in the past voluntarily. We should not be a prisoner of the past however and miss out on living in the present moment.

Even positive memories create suffering until we become detached from them. When we think about a pleasant event from the past, we experience the very non-existence of this event at this present moment. This experience of non-existence causes us to suffer and it prevents us from experiencing ourselves in the present moment.

When we are detached and aware we will not suffer from thinking, dreaming and worrying about the future and past. We will be unaffected by these mental activities.

Our mental activities are not wrong. However most of them are blown out of proportion. Our mind must relax and withdraw whenever it is not needed. Then we will enjoy life. Less thoughts make us more effective and powerful.

Simply shutting down our minds is not the answer to the problem. We need our minds to be alert and ready. We need a balance between our mind and our awareness and consciousness. Our mind must withdraw most of the time and our awareness and consciousness must move into the foreground most of the time.

We achieve this state of balance when we are in deep relaxation. Deep relaxation is different from sleepiness or daydreaming. It is a state of alertness yet low mental activity. Because of your mind's low frequency and few thoughts it can perform optimally. Our mind requires stillness to respond appropriately to any circumstance.

While the mind is one big part of our Self, our awareness is another important part. With the help of our awareness we slow down our mind. A person completely immersed in sensual perception has no mental suffering. Through feeling we detach from our identification with the mind. Our perceptions become immediate, clear and crisp.

Our mind is not always the best guide for our lives. We must allow our awareness and consciousness to take the lead and have our mind take on the tasks it is best equipped to tackle; which is efficient thinking.

Our mind is limited to what we have experienced in our lives up to this present moment. Our mind does not know anything other than what we have experienced and what we can infer and deduct from our past experiences. Our mind does have the capability to think logically and infer or deduct in order to make conclusions about truths we have never experienced and that are unrelated to anything we have experienced. However our mental faculties are limited. Our consciousness on the other hand is unlimited. Our consciousness is vast and deep, it has no boundaries. It is far beyond the realm of our ordinary perception. It is connected to our essence and to the essence of all that is. With practice we expand our consciousness to become powerful. Our consciousness must be the guide for our mind. When our consciousness takes the lead our mind will happily follow.

Our awareness is the non thinking observer of our Self and our consciousness is the non-thinking knower of our Self. Where the mind retreats consciousness emerges.

Both awareness and consciousness evolve over time through practice.

The Power of
Non-Resistance

*When we are non resistant we do not become free form
fear but we become free with fear. In non- resistance the
Self disappears. What remains is Consciousness*

To practice non-resistance is the fast track to a happy and successful life.

Non-resistance gets us unstuck whenever we cannot move forward. Non-resistance opens the doors to states of consciousness that we could not even imagine. Non-resistance disarms and transforms.

Non-resistance is the passive counterpart to intent and willpower. All aspects must work together in harmony. The state of non-resistance as a passive state is being initiated by our intent.

What exactly is it that we must be non-resistant about ?

The answer is we must be non-resistant to "Whatever Is".

To illustrate what non-resistance is, let us assume we are stressed because of our low bank balance. Being non-resistant to the fact that we have a low bank balance is not the answer. Facts are facts no matter how we feel about them. Instead we must be non-resistant to the reaction we have to our low bank balance. To be more precise, we want to be non-resistant to our perception of our reaction to our low bank balance.

Feelings are symptoms of our subconscious patterns and our state of consciousness. When we are aware of the force that causes our feelings to come to the surface we must practice non-resistance to this force. When we are non-resistant to the cause of whatever we feel and perceive, we detach and cease to identify ourselves with what we perceive.

At times we may sense a numb, undefined, latent feeling in us. This latent feeling grows into an acute feeling when it reaches the surface. For example we may have a latent feeling of anxiety. When this feeling is latent it influences our well being and our actions subconsciously. Latent feelings get triggered by external circumstances or by our thoughts and by our reactions to circumstances. We must become aware of these latent background feelings so that we are able to become non-resistant to them. Non-resistance will cause these feelings and patterns to weaken.

Non-resistance is not a moral imperative. We do not need to agree with whatever we are non-resistant to. To the contrary. Being non-resistant to a negative situation is the only logical response. Whatever situation exists, exists. Resisting the situation does not change anything about the situation. This does not mean that we must not change the circumstance or our feeling about it. There is nothing wrong with changing or avoiding what we don't like and there is nothing wrong with feeling bad about something we do not like.

However the problem is that we are not aware of the fact that it is our perception that causes our suffering. Once we realize this, our perception widens and our suffering disappears. We become detached from our reaction to the circumstance and begin to experience inner freedom.

In its highest state, non-resistance is a state of being. It does not need any reference point. Non-resistance does not require an object in relation to which it exists. Non-resistance is an independent state of consciousness.

We do not need to practice non-resistance to external circumstances. Rather we need to be non-resistant to our internal response to external circumstances. At a deeper level we realize that we do not have to be non-resistant to our internal response either but to our attachment to our internal response. Once we cease to attach our identity to whatever we experience internally and externally we are truly non-resistant.

Our internal emotional response to an external circumstance or thought cannot affect us as long as we are detached from our response. We must be aware of our response when it happens. In the state of non-resistance, our response to whatever is cannot affect our inherent state of inner peace.

People who have mastered non-resistance retain their emotional responses to external circumstances and thoughts. Just like any other person they feel anger, jealousy and stress. However they are not attached to these emotions and as such they do not suffer from them. They simply observe them as they come and go. There is no mental chatter or judgment about the perceived circumstances nor about their emotional response.

Therefore in the state of non-resistance we do not become free from fear but we become free with fear.

In the beginning non-resistance is experienced as a feeling. With practice it becomes a a state of consciousness. As a state of consciousness non-resistance is always there when it is needed. It will not have to be called or produced. All our actions and responses will arise out of non-resistance.

Being detached does not mean that we cannot enjoy and take ownership of what is happening. Through detachment we untangle our Self from the object of our perception and from our emotional response to our perception. We are able to perceive freely without the distorted perception that comes from relying on our inherent mind patterns. When we perceive without identifying ourselves with the object of perception on a mental level, we are able to connect with the essence of what we perceive and gain true wisdom about the object. Without the prejudice of our own limited perception we are open to receive the information that is inherent in the object of our perception.

Non-resistance reaches even deeper. It affects the root of our suffering. Non-resistance validates whatever is at the present as being real.

As such non-resistance prevents our mind to deny, suppress, enhance or crave what we experience at the present moment. This has the effect that we become detached from what we experience. When we are detached, whatever happens has no power over us. It simply comes and goes.

When we are resistant, our mind holds on to whatever we resist. Even if we try to change, deny or suppress what we experience, our mind holds on to it. When we are non-resistant there is nothing for our feeling to attach to, so it disappears. In a perfect state of non-resistance there is no Self that anything can attach to. Everything comes and goes and nothing causes permanent suffering because our perception of our Self is not there anymore.

We have given up resistance to our Self and as a result cease to suffer.

Non-resistance touches the very essence of who we are.

Formula:

<u>Self = Dysfunctional Mind + Resistance</u>

<u>Self – Resistance = Functional Mind + Consciousness</u>

Without resistance the Self disappears. What remains is consciousness.

We do not have to be non-resistant to the external circumstances. Being non-resistant has nothing to do with whether or not we act in a particular situation or what we will do about the external circumstance that triggered our response. It has to do with how we react. It determines the quality of our actions and responses.

To come back to our example about having anxiety because of our low bank balance, there would be no use to fight an internal battle of resisting our anxiety about our low bank balance. When we have anxiety we have anxiety. We have to accept this as a fact. We cannot wish away facts or wish away our feelings about facts. Our anxiety will go away faster if we do not hold on to it or try to fight it. In the state of non-resistance we are free from mental suffering and we become more efficient in resolving the external circumstance. Our mind will be clear and focused to find the solution. When we are calm and peaceful, our perception widens. Our widened perception can receive the right opportunities to resolve any given problem. Acting in a state of non-resistance is acting in a state of mental openness and agility. It allows us to use our perception to our maximum benefit.

Our non-resistance to our response to a circumstance causes an opening in us. Through that opening our natural inherent states of inner peace, love and joy emerge and we are much better equipped to tackle the external circumstance while saving ourselves a draining and exhausting internal battle.

Non-resistance makes us receptive to the lessons that are contained in difficult circumstances and it enables us to learn from them.

Difficult circumstances may appear to be obstacles in our lives, however they contain valuable messages that, if we understand them, accelerate our growth. Non-resistance enables our consciousness to receive and understand these lessons.

Practicing non-resistance can be the hardest thing to do. The reason is that we cannot do it with our mind. Once we have set the intent to be non-resistant we have to feel it with our senses rather than force it with our willpower.

I discovered a method that works for me.

Whenever I have trouble to be non-resistant I accept my inability to be non-resistant. This acceptance then is non-resistance.

I noticed that it does not matter on what level we enter into the state of non-resistance. If we cannot be non-resistant directly to a feeling or thought, we can be non-resistant to the fact that we are unable to be non-resistant. And if that does not work we can be aware that there is non-resistance to whatever is at the present moment, may that be our own inability to be non-resistant or anything else. We have to give up our expectation that non-resistance has to feel or be perceived a certain way. Giving up our concept of non-resistance propels us onto one of the deepest levels of non-resistance.

By approaching our resistance in this fashion, step by step we relax deeper and deeper. Eventually we will experience non-resistance on all levels of our being.

Michael Rinne

Resistance is created by our mind. The antidote to it is our sensory feeling. Feeling takes us out of our mind. The more we immerse ourselves in feeling the less we are resisting. Pure feeling and resistance cannot co-exist. Therefore in our exercises we use our mind only in the beginning of the exercise. We use it only when we form the intent to be non-resistant. Then we must let go of our intent and immerse ourselves into feeling.

There are circumstances when we cannot be non-resistant. In those cases we accept that we cannot be non-resistant and allow whatever we happens, including our resistance. There are circumstances where there is no time to be non-resistant. We may have to act right away. In pure action our mind is still and as is such naturally non-resistant.

I realized that there are different levels of non resistance that mirror the different levels of our Self.

There is the physical non-resistance on the level of our body. This I call relaxation. Then there is the experience we have when we are non-resistant. This is non-resistance on the level of feeling. Finally there is non-resistance as a state of consciousness.

To be completely non-resistant is one of the most difficult tasks. At the same time however it can be very easy. The key is how we approach non-resistance. As long as we equal our non-resistance with a particular feeling or experience we cannot remain non-resistant for long. It is the nature of any experience to dissolve after a certain time. We cannot feel relaxed, go with the flow of life and feel inner peace permanently.

To maintain the experience of non-resistance is impossible. However this is not necessary as the experience is only the symptom not its substance. Any experience we attempt to maintain our mind will eventually destroy. The reason is that our desire for the experience contains the seed for its destruction. As long as we continue our desire to be non-resistant we solidify the fact that we are not non-resistant further.

It is not the experience of non-resistance that matters
but rather the state of consciousness of non-resistance.

The key is to realize that there is no right or wrong feeling of non-resistance. Non-resistance can be experienced in many different ways. Some of them we may not recognize as non-resistance. While each experience of non-resistance is real, it is still an individualized expression of the absolute state of consciousness of non-resistance.

We must realize that all we need to do is, form the intent to be in the state of consciousness of non-resistance. Then this state of consciousness expresses itself in a multitude of forms depending on the circumstances we are in.

The state of non-resistance as such does not have any quality. While it is being experienced on our physical level, on the level of consciousness it is a pure state of consciousness and is not experienced. We should not be attached to how non-resistance should feel.

To illustrate this point let us assume we exercise non-resistance in our mediation practice. At first we feel very relaxed. Then we may feel expanded. We have less thoughts and we are going with the flow of whatever happens. This is a typical experience of non-resistance.

Soon however there will be resistance emerging in us. It may be thoughts of the like : "this experience will end soon and I want it to last". This is a typical feeling of resistance to what is at the present moment. The key is to form the intent to be in a state of non-resistance to whatever is. In this example when we feel that we become resistant to the anticipated ending of our relaxed state we must be aware of our initial intent to be non-resistant. Just like peeling the layers of an onion, if we cannot be non-resistant to our resistance to the ending of our relaxed state, we must be conscious of our state of consciousness that is already non-resistant to whatever is. On the level of consciousness we are always non-resistant it is up to us to realize that.

The power of non-resistance is in the fact that non-resistance requires barely any exertion of energy. It takes almost no effort to form the intent to be non-resistant on the level of consciousness.

The reason we don't need any effort or energy is that on the level of consciousness all states are caused by mere willful impulse. There is no mental friction and there are no obstacles on the level of consciousness.

Therefore once we realize that non-resistance is not to be practiced on the level of experience but must be initiated on the level of consciousness, the exercise becomes effortless. On the physical level non-resistance is being experienced in many different ways. No matter whether we experience non-resistance as being relaxed, going with the flow, or as a feeling of resisting, thinking, being stuck, doubting etc. it does not matter once we have initiated the state of consciousness of non-resistance. We must not be attached to the expression of the state of consciousness on the level of form. As long as we are aware of our state of non-resistance, any feeling and experience we may have on the physical level is ultimately an expressions of non-resistance.

It is powerful that we can remain in a state of non-resistance throughout our experiences in and out of physical and mental relaxation, in an out of pleasant and unpleasant feelings and experiences. None of these experiences affect or state of non-resistance. The state of non-resistance is free of attributes and once it has been caused by our intent and is being upheld by our awareness it expresses itself in a multitude of different experiences.

With practice, non-resistance becomes our natural state of mind and our first response in any circumstance. When we are non-resistant we are able to cease all the opportunities that are contained in the circumstances we are faced with in our lives.

Freedom from Judgment

To judge is natural and necessary. Circumstances have to be assessed and qualified as they stand in relationship to us. They may be judged as good, bad, helpful and so on. Judging is a part of our critical mind.

However judging becomes a problem when it causes us to suffer. Judging can cause emotional attachment to the object of our judgment and as such prevent us of experiencing what we perceive.

The act of judging is not the problem. Rather it is our attachment to our judgment that causes problems. We solve this problem by accepting our judging as a temporary reaction of our mind.

For example we may think that the weather is bad today. This thought is harmless as long as it will not trigger a long term negative feeling.

The key to judging is to allow judgment to be what it is and to let it go once it has served its purpose. We accomplish this by being non-resistant to our judgments. If we let our judgments be without trying to suppress, deny or indulge in them, our state of consciousness remains unaffected by our judgments.

The problem is that people suffer from their own judgments. We judge ourselves for judging others and we judge ourselves for judging ourselves. By being judgmental we get caught up in our emotions and feelings about our judgments. We lose the ability to let go of our judgments and therefore lose the ability to experience the present moment. We are caught in a mental cycle of judging. We either consciously or unconsciously suffer from this problem and as such miss out on life.

Being judged by other people and judging other people can be beneficial and harmful. Therefore we need to be careful how we express our judgments to other people. As long as we judge ourselves we will also be affected by other people's judgments. Once we allow ourselves to judge but avoid holding on to it, other people's judgments will no longer affect us. Then judgments will no longer derail our states of consciousness.

Once we taste the freedom and power of non-resistance to our judging we experience that we can be affected by judgment on one level and be completely unaffected on another level. It is liberating to allow oneself to judge and at the same time to not take one's judgment too seriously.

Especially in spiritual life there are many judgments. We judge what we should feel, what we should experience and what we do not experience but should experience. These judgments can be extremely destructive and hinder our spiritual growth.

It is fruitless to fight our judgments with our mind. Our mind can only attempt to suppress them. When we practice non-resistance to our judgments and to other people's judgments, they cease affect us.

In the beginning it is difficult to accept our judgments. However we can accept that we cannot accept our judgment. In focusing our awareness onto that acceptance, the judgment no longer bothers us. Step by step we become detached from all judgments.

Freedom from Limiting Concepts

Concepts are creations of our mind. As such they are highly individual and refer to our past experiences.

Concepts are pervasive in our lives. Even spiritual experiences such as love, inner peace or oneness become concepts when we label them as such.

When we attempt to re-experience a past spiritual experience we are chasing a concept. Granted there are remnants of physical remembering in us about the past experience. The physical remembering is not a concept.

As physical beings we store all our experiences in form of mental concepts in our mind.

For example when we imagine wealth, it is a concept until we experience it. Before that, the idea of wealth remains a concept. Any concept is flawed because it is relative to our patterns and our past experiences. In other words, what we may think of as wealth may be completely different from what another person thinks of as wealth.

There comes a point when we feel the urge to shed ourselves of our concepts, including our spiritual concepts. Unless we directly experience spiritual truths, there is no use in pursuing them. Even states of unconditional love, inner peace and joy are mere concepts as long as we are in pursuit of them.

When we let go of our concepts we begin to experience.

When we are able to let go of our concepts we fully experience whatever is at the present moment.

How do we go about letting go of our concepts ?

The key to letting go of concepts is not to resist them.

Once a concept has been formed it becomes part of our reality. There is no benefit in denying, suppressing or enhancing the concept. However we do not need to be attached to it. Concepts serve as guiding and organizing principles up to a certain point. However once we are on our path we must become detached from them in order to experience their inherent essence.

One of most pervasive, yet elusive concepts is that of our "Self".

The concept of our "Self" is our idea of who we perceive ourselves to be. Every minute we are awake we have a concept of who we are. Most people have never physically experienced who they are. Therefore everything we think about our Self is a mere concept.

Attempting to understand our "Self" is like a dog chasing his tail. We can never fully reach our "Self". That is because the "Self" itself is a concept. It only lives in our mind. Concepts are mind created and as such not based in reality. They cannot be experienced.

We are a mere concept and once we realize that this concept is relative and dependent on our limited past experiences, our perception of who we are will shift.

What lies underneath the concept of our Self cannot be put in words but can be experienced. One method to prepare ourselves to experience who we are is to let go of our concept of our "Self". We can accomplish this by becoming aware of our concept of our Self first and as second step practice non-resistance to the concept of our Self.

We do not need to deny, suppress or change the way we perceive our Self. In accepting our perception of our Self, we become detached from it. And because our Self is a mere creation of our perception we become detached from our Self itself. Our Self ceases to exist. What remains is consciousness.

When we become aware of our concepts we become detached from them. At that stage they will no longer prevent us from experiencing their inherent essence. Once we have developed our awareness we will cease to pursue concepts as concepts and access their inherent essence at all times.

Freedom from Limiting Concepts Exercise

The goal of this exercise is to experience freedom from our goals and concepts. All pressure that comes from our desire to accomplish our spiritual goals shall be lifted in this exercise.

Start with the 7 minute breathing exercise.

Breathing Exercise

Lay down or sit comfortably.

Close your eyes or leave them half way open whatever feels more comfortable.

Become aware of your breath. Do not actively focus on your breath. Be aware that there is breathing inside of you.

Breathe passively. Let the breathing happen and feel the air flowing through your body. Feel your body how it is being touched by your breathing.

Allow your breath to become subtle.

Now become aware of yourself observing your breath. Be aware of your awareness.

Relax and sink deeper. Relax deeper and deeper.

After 7 minutes slowly open your eyes and express gratitude for how you feel.

◆ ◆ ◆

After the seven minute breathing meditation do the Deep Relaxation Exercise for 5 minutes.

Deep Relaxation Exercise
Close your eyes again or leave them half open whatever feels more comfortable.

Relax your body.
Be aware of your body.

Shift your awareness to your feet.
Relax your feet.

Shift your awareness to your lower legs.
Relax your lower legs.

Shift your awareness to your upper legs.
Relax your upper legs.

Shift your awareness to your hips.
Relax your hips.

Shift your awareness to your lower back.
Relax your lower back.

Shift your awareness to your back.
Relax your back.

Shift your awareness to your shoulders.
Relax your shoulders.

Shift your awareness to your neck.
Relax your neck.

Shift your awareness to your upper arm.
Relax your upper arm.

Shift your awareness to your lower arm.
Relax your lower arm.

Shift your awareness to your hands.
Relax your hands.

Shift your awareness to your belly.
Relax your belly.

Shift your awareness to your chest.
Relax your chest.

Shift your awareness to your throat.
Relax your throat.

Shift your awareness to your lips
Relax your lips.

Shift your awareness to your nose.
Relax your nose.

Shift your awareness to your eyes
Relax your eyes.

Shift your awareness to your skull.
Relax your skull.

Shift your awareness to the top of your head.
Relax the top of your head.

Inhale deeply.
Hold your breath for 30 seconds then exhale and relax your entire body.

Again inhale deeply.
Hold your breath for 30 seconds then exhale and relax your entire body.

Feel your entire body relaxed.

Feel gratitude for being relaxed. Enjoy the feeling of relaxation and the feeling of gratitude.

Sink deeper and deeper.

If you are sleepy that is fine. You can take a nap.

If you feel you cannot relax do not force yourself. Accept that you cannot relax. And if you cannot accept that you cannot relax do not worry simply accept whatever is happening inside of you.

Be non-resistant to whatever you feel.

Do not expect any particular result from this exercise.

Sink deeper and enjoy your state. Nobody is judging you.

Relax deeper.

♦ ♦ ♦

After five minutes locate and be aware of a spiritual concept you may have. One of the concepts could be that you want to do this spiritual exercise successfully.

Another example of a concept would be, "I need to be relaxed, or I want to be loving, or I want to be liberated, or I want to be content, or I am not good, or I have too many thoughts" etc.

Be aware of your concept. Have an attitude of non-resistance towards it. If you cannot be non-resistant right now then do not resist that you cannot be non-resistant.

Give up everything you learned about being spiritual.

Give up your spiritual goals. Give up achieving anything in this exercise. Even give up your desire to be in the present moment.

Do not become too pushy wanting to give up. If you cannot give up then stay with it.

Feel how you sink deeper. Feel how you are peeling off layer upon layer of yourself.

Be aware that all your concepts are not real. You create them and you have the power to let go of them. Let go of them.

Then allow anything that happens to happen and enjoy allowing everything in a non-judgmental way.

Express gratitude.

If you notice any change in how you perceive make a note of it.

Conclude the exercise.

The Presence Formula
Introduction

Being in the present moment is a quality of being and as such a state of consciousness.

It is not about being present to a particular internal or external event nor does it have to do with time. Rather it is experienced as a state of consciousness.

To be present in a temporal sense is impossible. We will never be exactly at the point from where we could experience the present moment in a temporal sense. When we realize that we are present, the moment has passed already. We can never quiet grasp the present moment as it happens. In states of deep relaxation however we can experience complete presence as a state of mind.

When we cultivate presence as a state of mind we are able to be present to whatever moment unfolds without having to focus on any particular moment.

Presence occurs when our mind slows down. When our mental activity has been reduced to a minimum we experience more intensely what happens around us.

To achieve presence we should practice deep relaxation, non-resistance, non-judgment, letting go of mental concepts and gratitude.

In the state of presence our perceptions become clear and crisp and we become highly alert. There is no mental distraction. No energy is lost. We feel energetic and alive and we perceive this energy in everything we perceive.

In the state of presence we perceive the life energy in everything we encounter. This causes a virtuous cycle of perceiving and receiving this energy. Our perception of our feelings and of our "Self" becomes clear as it is filled with energy and knowing. In the state of presence we know who we are.

The Presence Formula

Formula: <u>Presence = Non-resistance to "what is" + Gratitude</u>

Presence is a quality of being that arises out of
non-resistance to "what is" combined with Gratitude

To practice presence means to accept the "what is". "What is" is that what we perceive and experience at any given moment. It includes external and internal realities.

Accepting external reality is the first step on the path to presence. As a second step we must become aware of our internal responses to the external realities. Once we are aware we must practice non-resistance to our internal responses.

In accepting our perception of our internal realities, our awareness sheds illuminates our perception and causes our perception to expand. This expansion of our perception causes our mind to withdraw and our thoughts to subside.

Attempting to reach the present moment with the help of our mind cannot work. Our mind understands presence only as a concept. Once we realize that we are always in the present moment, we reach presence. Once we drop the concept of the present moment and allow ourselves to feel and experience whatever is, we reach the present moment.

Experiencing the present moment means experiencing ourselves in the state of presence.

The practice of non-resistance combined with expressing gratitude are the fast track to the state of presence.

Gratitude prevents our mind to keep looking for the present moment. With the help of gratitude we are able to fully experience what is. Any experience that is fully experienced is experienced in the state of presence.

Our mind either rehearses the future or rehashes the past. Whenever we have an experience, our mind attempts to hold on to it. By doing so our mind prevents us from experiencing whatever is at the moment. With the help of gratitude we prevent our mind to hold on to what we experience. With gratitude we are be able to ride the moments as they come and go.

To accomplish what we want in life we have to start from where we are in order to get to where we want to go. In order to start from where we are we have to be aware of our current situation. In other words we have to be present. In order to be present we have to accept whatever is at the present moment. Acceptance comes with gratitude.

As long as we strive to be present we actually resist the present moment. Once we give up the concept of presence and realize that all we need to do is to be with what is we enter presence.

In one of my experiences of intense presence I remember that I was sitting in a chair for hours gazing at the white living room wall. I was completely immersed in my perception of the wall and amazed by the life I experienced in that wall. It was is if the wall was moving and I could feel the essence of it. The life in the wall was connected to the essence in me. After several hours I got up and walked outside the house and through the streets of the town in the part of India where I used to go every year to meditate. Every movement I made felt automatic and smooth. I experienced the people that passed by as being closely connected to me. I felt inner peace and causeless joy.

Later that day I felt my heart opening up wide. I felt compassion for all the people that passed by me. I felt connected to their essence. This essence I experienced as an inner truth about who we all are. Experiencing this common essence made everything else appear as if in a dream, almost unreal. My reactions to the people passing by were different than usually. Looking at the peoples' eyes caused my joy and compassion expand even further. I felt overpowered by the intensity of these feelings. I went home and sat for more to experience what was happening. I intensely felt connectedness and love.

The Presence Formula consists of two components. Non-resistance to what we experience and gratitude for what is. These are the two aspects we must cultivate. In the state of presence we experience and perceive everything around us as new, fresh and crisp. We feel connected with the essence of everything. We perceive this essence in all people and objects. We feel compassion for the suffering that is caused by us being excluded from this presence. We realize how much we have missed out on the joy of life.

Day 6 & 7

The Presence Formula Exercise

The goal of this exercise is to become present and to experience "what is". Presence is not understood as clock time but rather as a quality of being and a state of consciousness.

Do this exercise on day 6 and on day 7.

Seven minute Breathing Exercise
Lay down or sit comfortably.

Close your eyes or leave them half way open whatever feels more comfortable.

Become aware of your breath. Do not actively focus on your breath. Be aware that there is breathing inside of you.

Breathe passively. Let the breathing happen and feel the air flowing through your body. Feel your body how it is being touched by your breathing.

Allow your breath to become subtle.

Now become aware of yourself observing your breath. Be aware of your awareness.

Relax and sink deeper. Relax deeper and deeper.

◆ ◆ ◆

Deep Relaxation Exercise for five minutes

For 5 minutes do the deep relaxation exercise.

Relax your body.
Be aware of your body.

Shift your awareness to your feet.
Relax your feet.

Shift your awareness to your lower legs.
Relax your lower legs.

Shift your awareness to your upper legs.
Relax your upper legs.

Shift your awareness to your hips.
Relax your hips.

Shift your awareness to your lower back.
Relax your lower back.

Shift your awareness to your back.
Relax your back.

Shift your awareness to your shoulders.
Relax your shoulders.

Shift your awareness to your neck.
Relax your neck.

Shift your awareness to your upper arm.
Relax your upper arm.

Shift your awareness to your lower arm.
Relax your lower arm.

Shift your awareness to your hands.
Relax your hands.

Shift your awareness to your belly.
Relax your belly.

Shift your awareness to your chest.
Relax your chest.

Shift your awareness to your throat.
Relax your throat.

Shift your awareness to your lips
Relax your lips.

Shift your awareness to your nose.
Relax your nose.

Shift your awareness to your eyes.
Relax your eyes.

Shift your awareness to your skull.
Relax your skull.

Shift your awareness to the top of your head.
Relax the top of your head.

Inhale deeply.
Hold your breath for 30 seconds then exhale and relax your entire body.

Again inhale deeply.
Hold your breath for 30 seconds then exhale and relax your entire body.

Feel your entire body relaxed.

Feel gratitude for being relaxed. Enjoy the feeling of relaxation and the feeling of gratitude.

Sink deeper and deeper.

If you are sleepy that is fine. You can take a nap.

If you feel you cannot relax do not force it. Accept that you cannot relax. And if you cannot accept that you cannot relax do not worry simply accept whatever is happening inside of you.

Be non-resistant to whatever you feel.

Do not expect any particular result from this exercise.

Sink deeper and enjoy your state. Nobody is judging you.

Relax deeper.

♦ ♦ ♦

Now set your intent to be fully present and accept whatever is or happens right now.

Let go of judging, resisting and wanting.

Relax into whatever you perceive. For example you can focus and relax into your breath or be present to whatever you feel at this moment.

Feel whatever you feel and stay with it.   Fully experience it with your senses.

If your mind is running fast and you have many thoughts accept this as what is happening at the present moment. Your non-resistance will get you into the present moment.

If you cannot let go of your resistance then accept this also as what is happening in the present moment.

Do not resist the fact that you cannot resist. Just continue resisting and realize that this is what is happening at the present moment. Be detached from your resistance and do not judge yourself.

If you feel your mind quieting down and your senses becoming sharper be grateful for it. You are becoming present. Feel how it feels to be grateful. Feel how your gratitude is creating an opening for you to sink deeper into presence.

Be aware that you cannot search for the present moment. It does not exist in the future nor in the past. It is always already here. Even if you do not feel it. Your acknowledgment of it is sufficient for it to become reality.

If the feeling of presence does not fully emerge or if it quickly subsides do not try to hold on to it. Do not enhance or attempt to lengthen the duration of it. Simply experience whatever is at the present moment.

Do not resist anything not even your resistance.

If thoughts and emotions come, let them come. If you do not grasp or suppress your thoughts they will come and go. Be non-resistant to them.

Be non-judgmental to whatever happens. Let go of your expectations.

If thoughts come, let them come and let them go. Allow your awareness to rest on the thoughts and experience them as if they were tangible objects. Do not linger on the content of the thoughts. Accept your thoughts as what is in the present moment. Become fully present to whatever is. No need to accomplish anything. Let go of all the expectations you may have about this exercise.

Feel your realization that you are already fully and completely present. All it takes is your realization to experience it.

If you feel a shift inside or a rush of energy or inner peace or any other change take a note of it.

Open your eyes and look around the room. Objects may appear to be more clear, fresh and crisp. This is a result of your experience of presence.

Conclude the exercise.

The Oneness Formula
Introduction

In the state of oneness we become free from suffering and are able to harness the power to manifest.

Oneness is a state of consciousness that exists in the absence of duality. Duality as a mental concept requires an observer and an object that is being observed. Duality prevents the direct experience and direct knowledge. It requires us to interpret our perceptions with our limited mind. Duality causes separateness.

Duality is not negative per se. Duality is required for this world to exist. For the person who has experienced oneness, duality in its many expressions is what makes life enjoyable.

Our suffering is not caused by the existence of duality. It is caused by our attachment to it. The problem is our inability to take form for what it is. We believe in the form itself. This deprives us from experiencing the essence inherent in form.

We believe in separateness and wonder how we can connect with other people. He who is in oneness has shifted his awareness. In the state of oneness we experience the manifold manifestations of this world as expressions of the one and only essence.

When we experience form without attachment we fully enjoy what we perceive. In the state of oneness we connect with the essence of the object of our perception through our act of perceiving.

There are several levels of oneness. On the first level we are no longer the outside observers of ourselves. Our awareness has merged with our perception. As a result everything we perceive, we perceive directly without the filter of our mind.

For example when we look at a tree we no longer observe ourselves looking at the tree. We simply look at the tree. At the same time we are fully conscious of the act of looking. Our awareness is in the act itself. Our awareness has merged with the looking. The viewpoint of our awareness has shifted from being outside of ourselves to being inside of ourselves.

When the Buddha said, *"When I am walking, I am walking, when I am eating I am eating",* he described how his awareness was one with his actions.

The second level of oneness is being one with the essence in every person.

In my own experience I have felt the essence of other people when I perceived them. It can be described as a recognition of the other person's true identity beyond the person's appearance. In a second experience I recall that I felt my essence as one with the essence of the person next to me.

At this stage of oneness, we experience that we as individuals with our physical bodies, different personalities, viewpoints and perceptions, are a mere expression of our essence. This essence in us is the same essence we recognize in other people.

On a third level of oneness we recognize the essence in all the things and objects we perceive. Whatever we perceive, we experience with a heightened clarity. At this stage it seems as if we were looking at an object for the very first time. In my experience objects appeared to move closer to me and they appeared to be vibrating. This phenomenon is caused by our perception of the essence inherent in the object.

Once we merge with the essence of all that is we are one with every-thing. In my experience in that state there is no experience. It is a pure state of consciousness. There is nothing to be experienced.

After one of my experiences of oneness my perception shifted. I be-gan to experience myself as an expression of the one and all pervasive es-sence. I realized how close I already was to what I have always searched for, the essence of all; a place, from where there is nowhere to go.

We move in and out of the different states of oneness. There is no permanence. The more we experience oneness the more we will be able to enjoy the duality of this world.

The Oneness Formula

Formula: <u>Awareness +Act of Perception = Oneness with our Self</u>

*When our awareness is one with the act of perception we
are in oneness with our Self*

How do we achieve oneness ?

The ingredients to reach the state of oneness are non-resistance, gratitude, awareness and feeling.

We must merge our awareness with our perceptions and with our actions. When we bring our awareness inside and allow it to be aware of its oneness with our perception we have reached oneness with our Self.

In order to merge our awareness we must be aware of our awareness first. We all have awareness and we are aware of it to varies degrees. We usually are aware of our actions and perceptions. Awareness is thoughtless. It is pure observation without content. Only on the secondary level our thoughts are being engaged, when our mind engages with our perception in order to interpret that what our awareness has observed.

Usually we perceive our awareness as being outside from us looking inwards. Or we perceive it as inside of us looking outwards. In short we perceive our awareness as separate from us.

However once our awareness ceases to be separate from us and merges with whatever we perceive, think, or do, we are one with our Self. One with our Self does not require that there such a thing as a "Self". Our awareness must become one with our perception. We will then only see whatever we see and nothing else. No thoughts about us seeing what we see. No observing us seeing what we see. There is only pure experience of the act of seeing.

Once we experience oneness with our Self we will move to the next level. We will experience oneness with others. When we are one with others we are able to see through the veil of form of the other person into the person's essence. When we recognize this essence we move closer to our own essence. Recognizing the true identity of others helps us recognizing our own identity.

The method I use to become one with my Self is to merge my awareness with my perceptions and with my actions.

How do we merge our awareness with our act of perceiving or doing ?

The answer is with the help of our sensory feelings. To illustrate this point imagine you are looking at a flower. In the beginning your awareness is separate from the act of looking. You are still aware of our act of looking. The more you focus on the experience the more your awareness moves inwards towards the act of looking. The more intense your experience of our act of looking becomes the closer your awareness moves towards it and eventually it merges with it.

Once we perceive without thinking we are one with our Self. When we experience oneness with our Self and oneness with other people we recognize the essence in our Self and in other people.

Recognizing the essence in all we perceive is wisdom. It is the wisdom that enables us to manifest. In order to manifest we must understand the essence of what we intend to manifest.

The same principle applies to our feelings. For example when we feel anger or love, we must give up our observer role. There is no need to observe us experiencing anger or love. We simply want to feel angry or loving.

This principle applies to our thoughts as well. Thoughts can be felt. When we feel the thought without focusing on its content we access the inherent meaning of the thought. In other words we experience the essence of the thought. The essence of a thought is far more meaningful than its content.

In my experience when I applied this exercise to my thoughts I felt a physical expansion in my head. I felt completely filled with the essence of a certain thought. At some point in the exercise my awareness of the content of the word "love" disappeared and all I experienced was the feeling of love. These experiences occur regularly when our awareness has merged with the essence of the thought.

The essence of the thought may, but does not necessarily have to be congruent with the content of the thought. For example let us assume we experience the thought "wall". We may not have the experience of a wall. We may also use words of which we do not know the meaning and still be able to experience their essence.

Being one with our Self enables us to shape our thoughts with our intent and to manifest them into reality.

If we have a hard time giving up our observer role we must practice non-resistance. Once we completely merge with the act of whatever we do or perceive there will be no resistance. With the help of non-resistance we bridge the gap for our awareness to merge with our Self.

After we have experienced oneness with our Self we should express gratitude. This causes a positive pattern, and a pathway for spiritual growth.

More and more we will merge in and out of oneness in our daily lives. The more we are in oneness the more we will be able to enjoy our lives.

In spiritual practice we go through phases of experiencing and understanding external realities on different levels. When we turn our awareness inside, we experience the same truths in ourselves. The pendulum of external and internal perception shifts back and forth.

When we are in the present moment we are one with our Self. The principle of Oneness is the principle of presence perceived from a different angle.

Our awareness is the active aspect of consciousness. In other words it is the eyes of our consciousness. The more our awareness grows, the higher states of consciousness we will experience. Consciousness uses awareness to know itself.

In the state of oneness we realize the true nature of things.

In the state of oneness all our energies are directed towards manifestation.

The Power of Embodiment

*Where our awareness merges with our perception there
is embodiment.*

The state of embodiment is a state of physical expression of the state of oneness in our bodies. We become embodied after we have completely attained the state of oneness, have existed of the experience and find ourselves back in our physical bodies. It is a transformation of our being as it lives in the world of expression and form.

At this stage there is still an experiencer and an object to be experienced. The experiencer is our awareness and our feelings are the object of our experience. When we have fully immersed ourselves into oneness with our Self, we emerge from it in the state of embodiment. Embodiment is the physically experienced effect that the state oneness has on us.

Before we have merged into oneness we observe ourselves from a viewpoint that is separate from us. When we are embodied, our awareness has completely merged with our perception and action. Before oneness we perceive our feelings as being inside of us. We feel separate from our feelings. When we are embodied our feelings and experiences become our action. For example instead of feeling love, we are love. Instead of feeling our love expanding outwards towards the people we are expanding our loving Self towards the people. In short we shift from action to being.

Before we emerged out of oneness we had experiences of certain states of consciousness. When we are embodied we no longer have states of consciousness but rather are those states. This "beingness" increases our life energy. We no longer feel present but presence becomes an aspect of who we are.

In the state of embodiment we feel ready, confident and in charge of our feelings. We are in the driver's seat. By embodying our states of consciousness we intuitively act in the most beneficial way. We become the center of the energy from which everything emanates. In the state of embodiment we no longer experience our powers but rather become our powers.

I the state of embodiment our mind is our tool over which we have complete power. Our awareness is no longer the observer. It has merged with our Self. Whatever we do or feel, there is an inbuilt, inseparable awareness of it. There is no separation, we become our awareness itself. We embody our awareness; we are manifested awareness. The state of embodiment is an active state. It empowers us to be active in the world. Our being is radiating outwardly. Whatever we do we feel ready and empowered to do it with confidence and ease. We are beyond experiences, we simply are.

Day 8

The Oneness Formula Exercise

The goal of this exercise is to experience oneness with ourselves.

Seven minute Breathing Exercise
Lay down or sit comfortably.

Close your eyes or leave them half way open whatever feels more comfortable.

Become aware of your breath. Do not actively focus on your breath. Be aware that there is breathing inside of you.

Breathe passively. Let the breathing happen and feel the air flowing through your body. Feel your body how it is being touched by your breathing.

Allow your breath to become subtle.

Now become aware of yourself observing your breath. Be aware of your awareness.

Relax and sink deeper. Relax deeper and deeper.

♦ ♦ ♦

Deep Relaxation Exercise for five minutes
For 5 minutes do the deep relaxation exercise.

Relax your body.
Be aware of your body.

Shift your awareness to your feet.
Relax your feet.

Shift your awareness to your lower legs.
Relax your lower legs.

Shift your awareness to your upper legs.
Relax your upper legs.

Shift your awareness to your hips.
Relax your hips.

Shift your awareness to your lower back.
Relax your lower back.

Shift your awareness to your back.
Relax your back.

Shift your awareness to your shoulders.
Relax your shoulders.

Shift your awareness to your neck.
Relax your neck.

Shift your awareness to your upper arm.
Relax your upper arm.

Shift your awareness to your lower arm.
Relax your lower arm.

Shift your awareness to your hands.
Relax your hands.

Shift your awareness to your belly.
Relax your belly.

Shift your awareness to your chest.
Relax your chest.

Shift your awareness to your throat.
Relax your throat.

Shift your awareness to your lips.
Relax your lips.

Shift your awareness to your nose.
Relax your nose.

Shift your awareness to your eyes.
Relax your eyes.

Shift your awareness to your skull.
Relax your skull.

Shift your awareness to the top of your head.
Relax the top of your head.

Inhale deeply.
Hold your breath for 30 seconds then exhale and relax your entire body.

Again inhale deeply.
Hold your breath for 30 seconds then exhale and relax your entire body.

Feel your entire body relaxed.

Feel gratitude for being relaxed. Enjoy the feeling of relaxation and the feeling of gratitude.

Sink deeper and deeper.

If you are sleepy that is fine. You can take a nap.

If you feel you cannot relax do not force it. Accept that you cannot relax. And if you cannot accept that you cannot relax do not worry simply accept whatever is happening inside of you.

Be non-resistant to whatever you feel.

Do not expect any particular result from this exercise.

Sink deeper and enjoy your state. Nobody is judging you.

Relax deeper.

♦ ♦ ♦

Now focus on a feeling you encounter often. It can be your anxiety about finances, issues in a relationship or any other pleasant or unpleasant feeling.

Locate where you feel this feeling is in our body.

Once you located the feeling stay with it and experience it with your senses.

Be aware that you are observing both the feeling and yourself having this feeling. Be conscious of this awareness.

If the feeling does not fully emerge or if it quickly subsides do not try to hold on to it. Do not enhance or elongate it either. Simply experience whatever is at the present moment.

Do not resist the feeling. Let it be whatever it is. If you have to express the feeling that is fine. However there is no need to express it outwardly if you do not feel like it.

If thoughts and emotions come let them come. Do not grasp them and do not push them away. They will come and go. Be non-resistant to them.

Be non-judgmental to whatever happens and do not judge yourself. Let go of your expectations.

Feel how the initially dense feeling of suffering starts moving and rest your awareness on it.

Be grateful that you are aware of your feeling without being attached to it.

Be grateful for the feeling of your gratitude.

Now move your awareness closer and closer towards this feeling.

Visualize how your awareness is merging with your feeling.

Be non-resistant to whatever happens or does not happen. Be grateful that you have awareness and that it can merge with your feeling.

If thoughts come let them come. Rest your awareness on the thought and experience it as if it was a tangible object. Do not hang on to the content of the thought.

Become fully present with whatever is. No need to accomplish anything. Let go of all your expectations you may have about this exercise.

If you do not feel one with the feeling, feel whatever you feel and know that you are one with whatever is.

If you feel a shift inside or a rush of energy or inner peace or any other change take a note of it.

Conclude the exercise.

The Power of Embodiment Exercise

The goal of this exercise is to reach oneness with ourselves and feel how we are embodying our experiences and our feelings. We are no longer experiencing from a separate viewpoint. Instead we "are" what we feel. For example if we feel love, we are love and we express and spread love with whatever we do. In this exercise we shift from experiencing into being.

Seven minute Breathing Exercise
Lay down or sit comfortably.

Close your eyes or leave them half way open whatever feels more comfortable.

Become aware of your breath. Do not actively focus on your breath. Be aware that there is breathing inside of you.

Breathe passively. Let the breathing happen and feel the air flowing through your body. Feel your body how it is being touched by your breathing.

Allow your breath to become subtle.

Now become aware of yourself observing your breath. Be aware of your awareness.

Relax and sink deeper. Relax deeper and deeper.

◆ ◆ ◆

Deep Relaxation Exercise for five minutes
For 5 minutes do the deep relaxation exercise.

Relax your body.
Be aware of your body.

Shift your awareness to your feet.
Relax your feet.

Shift your awareness to your lower legs.
Relax your lower legs.

Shift your awareness to your upper legs.
Relax your upper legs.

Shift your awareness to your hips.
Relax your hips.

Shift your awareness to your lower back.
Relax your lower back.

Shift your awareness to your back.
Relax your back.

Shift your awareness to your shoulders.
Relax your shoulders.

Shift your awareness to your neck.
Relax your neck.

Shift your awareness to your upper arm.
Relax your upper arm.

Shift your awareness to your lower arm.
Relax your lower arm.

Shift your awareness to your hands.
Relax your hands.

Shift your awareness to your belly.
Relax your belly.

Shift your awareness to your chest.
Relax your chest.

Shift your awareness to your throat.
Relax your throat.

Shift your awareness to your lips.
Relax your lips.

Shift your awareness to your nose.
Relax your nose.

Shift your awareness to your eyes.
Relax your eyes.

Shift your awareness to your skull.
Relax your skull.

Shift your awareness to the top of your head.
Relax the top of your head.

Inhale deeply.
Hold your breath for 30 seconds then exhale and relax your entire body.

Again inhale deeply.
Hold your breath for 30 seconds then exhale and relax your entire body.

Feel your entire body relaxed.

Feel gratitude for being relaxed. Enjoy the feeling of relaxation and the feeling of gratitude.

Sink deeper and deeper.

If you are sleepy that is fine. You can take a nap.

If you feel you cannot relax do not force it. Accept that you cannot relax. And if you cannot accept that you cannot relax do not worry simply accept whatever is happening inside of you.

Be non-resistant to whatever you feel.

Do not expect any particular result from this exercise.

Sink deeper and enjoy your state. Nobody is judging you.

Relax deeper.

◆ ◆ ◆

Now focus on a positive feeling inside of you such as love, inner peace or compassion.

Locate where you this feeling is in our body.

After you have located the feeling stay with it and experience it with your senses.

Be aware that you are observing the feeling and yourself. Be aware of your awareness.

If the feeling does not fully emerge or if it quickly subsides do not try to hold on to it. Do not enhance or elongate it. Simply experience whatever is at the present moment.

Allow the feeling to be however it feels. If you want to express the feeling that is fine. However there is no need to express it.

You have activated your intent to locate and feel the feeling. Now all that is required from you is to stay with the feeling.

If thoughts and emotions come let them come. Be non-resistant to them.

Be non-judgmental to whatever happens and to yourself. Let go of any expectation.

Feel how your awareness of the feeling causes it to expand and become subtle.

Be grateful for feeling your gratitude in your body.

Now move your awareness closer and closer towards this feeling.

Visualize how your awareness is merging with your feeling.

Activate your intent for your awareness to merge with your feeling.

Be non-resistant to whatever happens or does not happen. Be grateful that you have an awareness and that it can merge with your feeling.

If thoughts come, let them come and let them go. Do not linger on the content of your thoughts.

Become fully present with whatever is. No need to accomplish anything. Let go of all the expectations you may have about this exercise.

If you do not feel one with the feeling feel whatever you feel and know that you are one with it. If you feel a shift inside or maybe a rush of energy or inner peace or any other change take a note of it.

Now feel that you are embodying your feeling. Your feeling is filled with your awareness and consciousness. You are no longer perceiving your feeling as separate from you. You are the feeling. If it is love that you feel then you are love or any other feeling you may have.

Feel your expanding power. You are whatever you are aware of. You now are the master of this feeling. You have the power to direct it, spread it wide, focus it on one particular person or simply observe yourself.

Feel how you affect everything you perceive with your state of being.

Take a note of how you feel. Conclude the exercise.

The Powerful Heart Formula

Formula : <u>oneness with all beings + recognition of the essence inherent in all beings = compassion</u>

When we are connected to the essence that is in all be-ings we feel compassion for all beings.

Our consciousness expresses itself in different ways on the physical level of which love and compassion are one of the most powerful aspects.

Love is an expressed state of consciousness. It has no negative or positive. It has no conditions or judgments. It is pure creative energy.

Love at its highest level is a state of consciousness. Expressed love is energy. We feel this energy when our physical and subtle bodies are receptive. Love cannot be caused by our mind.

Whatever the mind creates has two sides to it. Our mind cannot cre-ate without also creating its opposite.

When we are deeply relaxed and non-resistant, we cause an opening for love to emerge.

Romantic love is conditional. It requires a reason to exist.

For example if our romantic partner changes, our love may be replaced by disappointment. The disappointment was already inherent in the romantic love in latent form and becomes active when it gets triggered.

Love as an energy is free of conditions. It requires no justification to exist. Its natural state is expansion. In its expanded state it is compassion.

Love can be felt in many different ways. Sometimes we do not even recognize it as love. Therefore we must focus our awareness on the state of consciousness of love and avoid to be attached to its expressions in the physical world.

When we are aware of the essence of love, we will not misunderstand what love is. We avoid mistaking feelings for love that are not love and we will stop chasing love in its manifested forms. If we look for love in the world of form, we may find it. However many times over we will mistake what appears to be love for love.

In the state consciousness of love we emanate love as part of our being. When our bodies are cleared of all friction and blockages, this state of consciousness expresses itself in our bodies and flows through our bodies as energy, emanating outwardly.

On the physical level love has to expand and flow uninterrupted. Whenever it is blocked we experience it as suffering. In being non-resistant to whatever we feel we allow love to flow freely.

It is the inherent nature of love to flow, expand and unite with itself. When we ride the energy of love we move onto the levels of consciousness where creation occurs.

All our actions and reactions are expressions of love. Sometimes we do not recognize the love in them, however when we are recognize the love as the energy within all actions we begin to recognize it everywhere.

To illustrate that love is within all actions let us look at how money works in our lives. We give and receive money because of love. When we buy ourselves a nice car or a beautiful dress, we do this to feel loved by other people. We spend money to receive love in all its varies forms. Even spending money on groceries is to nurture our body which is nothing other than receiving love from food. When we receive money we feel loved. When we do not receive money we feel unloved.

Often the love is hidden in our actions and we do not recognize it as such. When we open our inherent source for love, our actions begin to reflect the love. We become wiser in our actions. Our actions will not be driven by our wanting of love. We will not do things in order to receive love. We will not withhold love either. We will not waste money to buy us love and so on.

A loving person does not need to act or react a certain way to receive love. The loving person always acts out of abundance. There is no feeling of lack.

The loving person radiates causeless love outwardly. People feel this love and are drawn to this kind of person.

In the example of money, the loving person will always have the advantage over the non loving person. People want to be around loving people. People will consciously or unconsciously give money to the loving person in order to receive his or her love. The loving person will not waste money. Knowing that money cannot buy love, the loving person will not spend more money than is necessary. The loving person has no craving for love.

To realize how much our actions are driven by our wanting for love we should observe ourselves while we spend and receive money. We may notice that many of our actions are irrational and driven by our wanting for love.

We should not attempt to become loving for the purpose of receiving the love from other people. This attempt would condition our love. When we open the gates for our own unconditional love to flow freely, we will not crave love from anybody any longer. All we want is to give love. We will cease to equal material things with love. Our desires for material things will lessen. The object of our desire will lose its power over our state of happiness. We will enjoy the objects of our desires as long as we have them. When we lose them we remain happy.

Our stream of love makes us detached from material things. We freely enjoy what we have and we successfully acquire whatever we like.

Love is powerful. It is the force of creation.

When we are completely filled with love, we are free from the mind. In the absence of the mind there is no friction and there are no obstacles to block the creative force of love.

Love is the creative aspect of our consciousness. In order to master the art of manifestation we have to understand love on the level of consciousness. When we rest our awareness on love as a state of consciousness we access love in its highest form. We must let go of our concepts of love to be ready to experience its many different expressions.

The Power of Compassion

Compassion is love in its expanded form.

Once we had the experience that we are one with all people, we begin to feel connected with all people. We are connected to the essence in all people and we witness the suffering around us. This suffering is caused by the people's wanting, the people' fear and by their ignorance of their true essence.

In my own experiences I felt compassion as a painfully sweet unconditional love for all life forms.

We feel compassion for ourselves, for our striving and suffering and for who we are. Compassion arises out of our recognition of our inherent essence. It is the realization of who we are.

Compassion has to expand and must be expressed. Once compassion has begun to flow, it cannot be stopped. Blocking the flow of compassion would cause suffering and create problems in our lives.

All compassionate actions have a powerful impact. The person who expresses and acts out of compassion receives an abundance of love in return. The fastest path to joy of life, happy relationships and material success is the path of compassion.

Compassion causes us to help other people. When we help people become free from their sufferings, it enables us to become free from our own suffering. Helping others becomes our natural state and we realize it as a necessity for our own well growth.

The Powerful Heart Formula Exercise

The goal of this exercise is to experience love and compassion and to feel how it expands in and beyond our bodies.

Do this exercise on day 10 and day 11.

Use a timer to time the intervals of the exercise.

Seven minute Breathing Exercise
Lay down or sit comfortably.

Close your eyes or leave them half way open whatever feels more comfortable.

Become aware of your breath. Do not actively focus on your breath. Be aware that there is breathing inside of you.

Breathe passively. Let the breathing happen and feel the air flowing through your body. Feel your body how it is being touched by your breathing.

Allow your breath to become subtle.

Now become aware of yourself observing your breath. Be aware of your awareness.

Relax and sink deeper. Relax deeper and deeper.

◆ ◆ ◆

Deep Relaxation Exercise for five minutes
For 5 minutes do the deep relaxation exercise.

Relax your body.
Be aware of your body.

Shift your awareness to your feet.
Relax your feet.

Shift your awareness to your lower legs.
Relax your lower legs.

Shift your awareness to your upper legs.
Relax your upper legs.

Shift your awareness to your hips.
Relax your hips.

Shift your awareness to your lower back.
Relax your lower back.

Shift your awareness to your back.
Relax your back.

Shift your awareness to your shoulders.
Relax your shoulders.

Shift your awareness to your neck.
Relax your neck.

Shift your awareness to your upper arm.
Relax your upper arm.

Shift your awareness to your lower arm.
Relax your lower arm.

Shift your awareness to your hands.
Relax your hands.

Shift your awareness to your belly.
Relax your belly.

Shift your awareness to your chest.
Relax your chest.

Shift your awareness to your throat.
Relax your throat.

Shift your awareness to your lips
Relax your lips.

Shift your awareness to your nose.
Relax your nose.

Shift your awareness to your eyes
Relax your eyes.

Shift your awareness to your skull.
Relax your skull.

Shift your awareness to the top of your head.
Relax the top of your head.

Inhale deeply.
Hold your breath for 30 seconds then exhale and relax your entire body.

Again inhale deeply.
Hold your breath for 30 seconds then exhale and relax your entire body.

Feel your entire body relaxed.

Feel gratitude for being relaxed. Enjoy the feeling of relaxation and the feeling of gratitude.

Sink deeper and deeper.

If you are sleepy that is fine. You can take a nap.

If you feel you cannot relax do not force it. Accept that you cannot relax. And if you cannot accept that you cannot relax do not worry simply accept whatever is happening inside of you.

Be non-resistant to whatever you feel.

Do not expect any particular result from this exercise.

Sink deeper and enjoy your state. Nobody is judging you.

Relax deeper.

◆ ◆ ◆

Now become aware of the location around your heart. It is the entire area in the middle of your chest.

Relax into whatever you feel.

Keep your awareness onto the heart area.

Now remember a moment when you felt love. Remember how it felt. Do not focus on the event, focus on the feeling you had. Feel it as if it was there right now.

Keep focusing on your heart area in your body.

Visualize your heart area how it expands. With every exhale your heart area and the feeling of love expands wider and wider in your body.

It expands and engulfs your head and your entire body.

Let the feeling expand further beyond your body. Feel how it fills the room.

Let it flow. Do not grasp it. Just experience.

Don't judge yourself. No expectations. There is nothing to accomplish.

Be grateful for whatever you feel. Become aware of your feeling of gratitude. Feel how your gratitude expands your feeling of love.

Slowly open your eyes. Look around the room. Notice how you feel and how you perceive now.

Take a note about your feeling and your perception.

Conclude the exercise.

The Detachment Formula

Formula: <u>Consciousness + Awareness + Intent = Self Realization</u>

*When our consciousness realizes itself with the help of
its awareness it is self realized*

Spiritual practice is the striving towards an envisioned goal and working towards becoming something we aspire to be.

We may reach a point where we become frustrated about our desire to reach our spiritual goal and want to give up and renounce all our spiritual goals. Despite how it feels, this phase of renunciation is very beneficial and often marks the start of a new phase of growth.

If we feel like giving up we should allow this feeling to unfold.

It is our natural desire to experience our being in complete renunciation. In the sate of renunciation we experience a subtle but powerful opening in ourselves. Other than openings in our hearts for example, this opening is not anticipated nor experienced in a traditional way. It is a subtle but powerful shift on the level of consciousness.

With the help of this shift we enter a higher state of consciousness. On the level of consciousness there are no experiences to be had. On the level of consciousness there is only realization. There is no becoming, no space, no dimension, and no time. There is only being.

In the state of complete non-resistance we shift into our own consciousness. Shifting is an instant switch from one level of consciousness to the next level without exertion of energy and without traveling any distance. It is beyond time and space. Shifting is the way the different aspects of consciousness merge in and out of focus of our awareness. While all aspects of consciousness exist at all times, what shifts is our awareness. It is as if the different aspects of our consciousness are shifting in and out of the spotlight of our awareness.

I remember one day I was meditating in the temple. Before I realized that I had shifted to another level I experienced a state of complete halt. I become completely detached from what I was doing and thinking. I was completely passive.

After the shift happened, it took some time to let my new state sink in and stabilize. Shifting to me feels like a physical and biological process that takes place in ones brain rather than a mental or cognitive process.

To bring about this kind of shift requires complete and utter renunciation of everything that has meaning to us.

After I experienced the shift I remember perceiving everything around me in a more subtle way. There was a certain softness to everything I saw and heard. I experienced inner peace and detachment from my thoughts. Some time later stronger feelings of compassion and love emerged.

The experience of a shift made me realize that spiritual growth is not about the spiritual experiences we have but about that what causes our experiences. It is about becoming aware of or consciousness.

Once we become detached from our desires for spiritual experiences we become liberated from our mental concepts as well. Once we are free from our concepts, our awareness will shift its focus towards our consciousness. The more awareness is directed towards our consciousness the more we will experience our true identity.

Spiritual experiences should serve as pointers on our path to our consciousness and not be our main focus.

Experiences are the expressions of our consciousness on the physical level. As long as we are attached to the expression of our states of consciousness we are attached to their manifestation in the world of form and we cannot realize the states of consciousness themselves.

Everything in this world is conditional and temporary. Whatever expression our state of consciousness takes in this world is dependent on the form we are in right now. For example when we feel compassion, we experience the expression of the aspect of consciousness that is compassion. How compassion is experienced is different for every person and depends on the person's individual, social and cultural conditioning.

Therefore the expressions of our states of consciousness in this world only serve as pointers. They tell us about the existence of the state of consciousness without revealing their true essence.

We should not be attached to any particular experience. It is important to be open to experiences without prejudice and preconception. An aspect of consciousness is being experienced in many different ways depending on our circumstances.

The different aspects of consciousness can only be realized with the help of our awareness. Our awareness is the part of our consciousness that knows itself. On the level of consciousness knowing replaces experience.

The more I entered my consciousness with my awareness I realized that I have the power to cause a certain aspect of my consciousness to unfold with the help of my intent.

Because there is no friction on the level of consciousness there is no lost energy and no effort and the aspects of our consciousness can be caused by our mere intent. For example my intent to be happy caused instantly my awareness of me as a happy being which was quickly followed by my physical and emotional experience of happiness.

The different aspects of consciousness are aspects of the one all encompassing consciousness. This all encompassing consciousness is the essence of all that is. It knows itself through the eyes of our awareness. It manifests through our intentional impulse. These three aspects of the essence; i.e. beingness, knowing and creating are the trinity of the essence.

We are an expression of this trinity. Once this truth has trickled down through the layers of our bodies, we experience this truth as it unfolds in the physical world. Until then our limited state of consciousness in the here and now does not know that it already knows about itself on its highest level.

By contemplating on this aspect, we direct our awareness into right direction. With our intent we cause our consciousness to know itself through its awareness. When we practice non-resistance, this knowing of its own being will be experienced by us on the physical level. When we intent for certain things to happen and they do not happen it is not because our intent was not strong enough but it is because there are obstacles caused by our mind that prevents the intended reality from manifesting in form.

Michael Rinne

On the level of consciousness there is no friction. All intentional impulses become instant reality.

On the level of consciousness we have already mastered the art of manifestation. However our mind does not know this yet.

If for example we intent to be aware of the aspect of love on the level of our consciousness we may not feel any love in our body. This is because we expect to experience love in a certain way.

The answer is to let go of our initial intent as soon as we have formed it and to not expect a certain outcome. If we are attached to experience love in a certain way we may miss experiencing it altogether.

When we are aware that we cause our states of consciousness all the time, we begin to experience their expression on the level of our physical bodies.

When all the levels of our self are in a state of non-resistance, our intent instantly causes us to experience the state we intended to manifest.

For example if we intent to be joyful we instantly feel joy. If we intend to feel wealthy we instantly feel wealthy.

In the beginning we may not know how to direct our awareness onto our consciousness. The key is to form the intent to do so and then be allow for it to unfold. On the level of consciousness our intent is being heard and answered.

We will realize that there is no separation between us and our consciousness. The entire process is taking place inside of us. Words are only pointers for us to keep our focus on what is important on the spiritual path. However we have to realize for ourselves who we are.

All manifestation is being initiated on the level of consciousness. Everything first becomes reality on the level of consciousness.

For reality to manifest in the physical world, there must not be any friction in ourselves. Friction exists on the level of our mind and is caused by our fear, denial, wanting and concepts. Once those obstacles are cleared, the reality we cause on the level of our consciousness manifests in our physical world effortlessly.

On the level of consciousness everything is being created out of abundance and not out of scarcity. Therefore whenever we focus on our wanting we fail. Wanting something implies its non-existence. We cannot manifest from a standpoint of non-existence. Realizing that everything is already in existence on the level consciousness and that all we have to do, for our intent to manifest itself, is to be receptive, enables us to master the art of manifesting.

The Detachment Formula Exercise

The goal of this exercise is to renounce all our goals. Eventually we shall drop the goal for this exercise as well.

Do this exercise on day 12 and day 13.

Use a timer to time the intervals of the exercise.

The exercise will be fourteen minutes.

Seven minute Breathing Exercise
Lay down or sit comfortably.

Close your eyes or leave them half way open whatever feels more comfortable.

Become aware of your breath. Do not actively focus on your breath. Be aware that there is breathing inside of you.

Breathe passively. Let the breathing happen and feel the air flowing through your body. Feel your body how it is being touched inside by your breathing.

Allow your breath to become subtle.

Now become aware of yourself observing your breath. Be aware of your awareness.

Relax and sink deeper. Relax deeper and deeper.

◆ ◆ ◆

Deep Relaxation Exercise for five minutes
For 5 minutes do the deep relaxation exercise.

Relax your body.
Be aware of your body.

Shift your awareness to your feet.
Relax your feet.

Shift your awareness to your lower legs.
Relax your lower legs.

Shift your awareness to your upper legs.
Relax your upper legs.

Shift your awareness to your hips.
Relax your hips.

Shift your awareness to your lower back.
Relax your lower back.

Shift your awareness to your back.
Relax your back.

Shift your awareness to your shoulders.
Relax your shoulders.

Shift your awareness to your neck.
Relax your neck.

Shift your awareness to your upper arm.
Relax your upper arm.

Shift your awareness to your lower arm.
Relax your lower arm.

Shift your awareness to your hands.
Relax your hands.

Shift your awareness to your belly.
Relax your belly.

Shift your awareness to your chest.
Relax your chest.

Shift your awareness to your throat.
Relax your throat.

Shift your awareness to your lips
Relax your lips.

Shift your awareness to your nose.
Relax your nose.

Shift your awareness to your eyes
Relax your eyes.

Shift your awareness to your skull.
Relax your skull.

Shift your awareness to the top of your head.
Relax the top of your head.

Inhale deeply.
Hold your breath for 30 seconds then exhale and relax your entire body.

Again inhale deeply.
Hold your breath for 30 seconds then exhale and relax your entire body.

Feel your entire body relaxed.

Feel gratitude for being relaxed. Enjoy the feeling of relaxation and the feeling of gratitude.

Sink deeper and deeper.

If you are sleepy that is fine. You can take a nap.

If you feel you cannot relax do not force it. Accept that you cannot relax. And if you cannot accept that you cannot relax do not worry simply accept whatever is happening inside of you.

Be non-resistant to whatever you feel.

Do not expect any particular result from this exercise.

Sink deeper and enjoy your state. Nobody is judging you.

Relax deeper.

◆ ◆ ◆

Now become aware of your goals. Pick a particular goal. It may be a material goal, a relationship goal or even a spiritual goal.

Now give up that goal. Start by saying to yourself that you are giving up this goal.

Now activate your intent to give up your spiritual goals. Your material goals. Your relationship goals.

The next step is to give up the goal to give up your goals. If you cannot give up this goal then give up whatever your goal is right now.

Renounce all that is. Do not care about anything that is.

There is nothing to care about right now.

It doesn't matter who you are, what you are doing and why you are doing this exercise.

Nothing matters. You just are.

Internalize these words:

I don't want to go anywhere.

I don't want to do anything.

At this stage if you are relaxed you are relaxed, if not you are not. You simply don't care.

You also don't care if you care or not, nothing is important now.

Repeat renouncing everything.

All you have to do is stay with what. i

Do not feel you are doing this exercise. Let it be done with you. You have given up taking any part in what is going on.

Conclude the exercise.

Book II

Introduction

The first book focused on the deconstruction of ourselves. This was necessary to free ourselves from limiting patterns, viewpoints and perceptions. The goal was to cultivate non-resistance and to experience the present moment in order to uncover our inherent creative powers.

In the second book we will learn how to re-construct ourselves in a way that enables us to manifest what we want in our lives.

Manifesting Pre-Requisites Introduction

At first our focus will be on manifesting emotions such as happiness and contentment. These are internal states that are more readily available than feelings in our physical body and external realities such as relationships and wealth.

Our inner emotional states are more fluid than external states and as such easier to manifest. If we have experienced oneness with ourselves in the first book it will require little effort to manifest our emotional states now.

In the second step the focus will be on manifesting bodily states, such as manifesting a pain free body. We will learn how to access our body intelligence.

In the third step the focus will be on manifesting external realities such as good relationships. The goal is to practice the skills necessary to manifest for example, a particular job, a desired relationship or financial wealth. Manifesting external realities is the most difficult level because it requires that we have experienced oneness with other people and oneness with everything. It is required that we have deep experiential understanding of love as a creative force. It is also required that we understand the "Space" in which everything is taking place.

Visualization is the technique we use to manifest. Visualization prevents our mind to create obstacles. We will manifest from a state of abundance and not from a state of wanting. When we visualize, we do this with the realization that everything we desire already exists on the level of consciousness.

Visualization will only work if our physical, emotional and spiritual bodies are prepared properly. Therefore we must continue to deconstruct and let go of our old patterns.

The three aspects of manifesting are sensory feeling, visualization and awareness. We must feel what we visualize as being real. The more real our vision is the more effective it is.

At first our subconscious will work against us. Whenever we desire something our subconscious causes a reality of scarcity of the very thing we desire. For example when we desire to have a car, our subconscious will focus on the fact that we do not have a car and as such it solidifies the non-existence of it. To overcome this dilemma, we need to fully understand our subconscious and use it to our advantage.

When we focus on our feeling about our vision and are present to our vision we will overcome our subconscious. The intense feeling about our vision combined with our realization that everything we desire is already in existence on the level of consciousness keeps our subconscious disengaged.

Why Visualization works

Why does visualization work ?

The answer is that with the help of visualization we create an internal reality. Vision implies that we already have what we want. Vision reinforces the principle that everything is already created on the level of consciousness. When we express this principal we enable it to become reality on the physical level as well.

Focusing our awareness on our vision works the same way as focusing on any other external object. Our vision should be as clear as a photograph. Once our vision stands, it does not need mental activity to exist. Because our vision is independent of our mind it is not exposed to the forces of our subconscious.

First we use our mind to initiate our vision. Once the vision has been created it remains in existence with the help of our perception. It becomes an independent reality. It is important to let go of our intent once our vision has been created.

We should experience our vision as clear and detailed as we experience any other externally image. Once we are aware of our vision, our mind withdraws and our feelings emerge. Once our vision has separated itself from our mind, our awareness begins to rest on our vision.

For example when we look at a tree, we are able to rest our aware-ness on the tree without effort. Our mind does not have to uphold our im-age of the tree because we easily recognize the tree as reality. All we do is observe the tree. Our subconscious is not involved. The same principle we must to use when visualizing.

When we create our vision we only use our mind in the beginning. All we need our mind for is to initiate our vision.

For example let us assume we want to have a new car. We use our intent to create the vision of the car we desire. Once we clearly see all the details about the car, we must let go of our intent. We need to let go of our wanting to create the vision of the car. In order to keep up the vision and keep it clear and real, instead of continuously engaging our mind, we must rest our awareness on the image of the car.

In this example we may want a certain car but in truth what we re-ally want is recognition or love. The essence of our desire will reveal it-self when we visualize our desire and we observe our feelings. We must learn to listen to our feelings in order to understand what we truly desire. Focusing on our true desires will always trigger intense feelings.

Sometimes we may not have a strong feeling about our vision. One reason may be that we focus more on the non-existence of what we want than its existence. Without realizing it, we experience the non-existence of what we want. For example if we attempt to visualize that we receive a large amount of money but feel very poor at the moment, our vision can-not work.

In situations where our focus on the non-existence of what we de-sire is too strong we use the technique of visualizing in stages. The first step is to acknowledge our current situation and be non-resistant to it.

For example if we want money because we are poor, we must first ac-knowledge that we are poor and we must not resist this feeling. Our non-resistance will eventually cause an opening in us. Now we shift our focus on being free from poverty. Once our feeling about our poverty has sub-sided, we become detached. Our initial fear of poverty has disappeared. We relax, become fearless and cease to feel poor. At that stage we are ready to focus on our vision of wealth.

Once we have a clear vision and an intense feelings about our vision we must send out the vision to our consciousness.

Clarity of Vision

For manifesting to work it is important that we see in detail what we are visualizing and we must be very clear about why we want it.

When we create our vision we have to visualize the image as detailed as possible. Incomplete visions are not perceived as real and thus discarded by our subconscious. Incomplete visions do not trigger the same intense feelings in us that are required for our manifestation to work.

For example if we desire to have a white Porsche 911 we must visualize a white Porsche 911. We should see and experience the color, the tires, the interior and ourselves in the picture. We must feel how it is to sit in the Porsche and drive it.

Our awareness does not differentiate between internal and external images. For our awareness our vision is as real as any external image. The mind on the other hand interprets certain perceptions to be more real than others. Therefore for our mind to support us in our exercise, it is very important that our vision is clear.

When we visualize, there is no need to artificially create feelings. In the state of non-resistance whatever we feel at the moment is the appropriate feeling, because it is the expression of the state of consciousness of our desire.

The clearer our vision is the less resistance we feel. Our vision unfolds the best when we are non-resistant. A clear vision prevents our mind to attempt to uphold and continuously recreate our vision. As long as we are still creating the vision we remain in our mind and our subconscious is dominant. Once the vision stands we must let go of it and simply experience it.

We must know why we want what we want. Our motivation must be free from conditions, justifications or judgments. For example if we want to own a large mansion, we should base our intent on the positive feelings we have when we live in the mansion and avoid any condition or judgment about our desire.

For example to justify our desire by thinking: "I want this mansion so I can impress my friends or so I do not feel so unhappy", is counterproductive. Justifying our desire such as: "I want this mansion because I have done so many good deeds and helped so many people": will harm our vision as well. We should not judge ourselves for wanting something. For example we may think: "I want the mansion and if I get it I will remain a humble person" Conditions, judgments and justifications engage our mind. They prevent our creative forces to unfold. They create a complicated mental relationship between us and our desire. If we desire to be humble or help many people we should simply focus on this vision without attaching it to the vision of the mansion.

The concepts we use to justify our desires are not helpful in the creative process.

Our motivation must be based on the positive reality of what we desire versus on its non-existence. For example if we want a mansion we should want it because we love the feeling that we have thinking about owning the mansion and not focus on our negative feeling of not yet owning the mansion at this time. Visions are not there to overcome negative circum-stances but to create positive realities.

However this does not mean that we should ignore the circumstances that we are in at this moment. To the contrary we must be aware of where we stand right now. If we have feelings of lack or poverty for example we should first focus on being free from it. Once this feeling has vanished we are ready to positively engage our creative forces to manifest.

Conditioning our Vision

We should avoid to condition our vision.

For example if we visualize that we are wealthy, we should simply enjoy the feeling of being wealthy without attaching a condition or justification to our vision. For example we want to be wealthy so we can help many poor people. If we enjoy being wealthy and also love to help poor people then there is no problem. In this case the vision of being wealthy and to help poor people is one vision.

Our judgments, justifications and conditions limit the power of our vision. They are dependent on our values. We all have different values upon which we base our judgments. Even though we share common societal values, because we only perceive the world through our own lenses, our judgments, justifications and conditions are relative to our individual circumstances. Our personality has been shaped by how we were brought up and by our experiences. Our judgments, justifications and conditions change through time as we ourselves change and gain new experiences. Our limited concepts about the world have been created by our mind that continuously interprets our experiences and our perceptions by using our subconscious patterns as reference points.

Our vision must be absolute and not relative. It must be free from our concepts. There should be no good nor bad in our vision.

We should chose that kind of vision which triggers the strongest possible feeling in us. For example if we desire to have a lot of money so that we can help many people, we must recognize which part of this two pronged desire is stronger. Then we separate the two desires and focus on the stronger desire first. For example if being wealthy triggers the strongest feeling, we should focus on this desire first. If helping people is a lesser i.e. a second degree desire we should separate it from the stronger desire. Otherwise the lesser desire will deplete our energy and take our focus away from our stronger desire. For example if we love to have a luxurious house and we also enjoy to do spiritual work, we should focus on living in the luxurious house first because by focusing on the strongest desire we free our positive creative feelings. After we have completed our focus on our strongest desire we will have unleashed tremendous creative energy that we can then use to focus on our second degree desire.

Lesser desires are often disguised conditions, justifications and even subconscious objections. When we focus on the lesser desire, our awareness will reveal their true essence. We may discover that a lesser desire is not a desire at all but a mental concept to justify a stronger desire. For example a concept could be that "only humble people should be wealthy" therefore we desire to be humble in order to justify our desire to be wealthy. Once we know the true nature of our desire we can drop the desire, alter it or let it develop independently without having to serve as a justification for another desire. For example if we discover that we have no strong desire to be humble, we simply drop this desire. When we stop being attached to the concept disguised as a desire, it will transform into a true desire. A true desire could for example be that instead of being good and humble we want to be significant and important and use our status to help many people in need.

Manifest in the Now

Always visualize in the presence. Perceive the object of your vision as if it was already in existence. If we project our vision into the future we engage our mind. The future is a mental concept. When we envision something to happen in the future our subconscious will solidify its non-existence in the now.

Our awareness cannot rest on something that we do not perceive as real. In essence we would do the opposite of creating our vision. Future is a concept of our mind. It is an obstacle to manifestation.

The future prevents us from experiencing our vision as present reality. Our awareness and our feelings do not know the concept of future. Either our vision is real or it is not.

Certain events must however occur in the future. For example if we want to visualize that we will graduate with high honors from college and our graduation date is in the future there certainly needs to be an element of future. Or for example we want to travel to a foreign country next summer. In these two examples future does not have to be a limiting factor. To handle the concept of future in these examples it is sufficient to focus on our vision and on the feeling it triggers as if we were at the graduation ceremony right now. In the example of traveling to a foreign country next summer, instead of using the future, we include into our vision that it is summer and we focus on how it feels traveling in the summer as if it was happening at this very moment.

Another technique to include time into our vision is to visualize the particular day and month on the calendar. For example if we want to travel on August 9, 2018 to Africa, we visualize seeing this date on the calendar. Visualizing the date on the calendar is being experienced as a present moment reality.

When using future we must be carful to allow our awareness to fully experience the vision as a present moment reality. Not only is the future a powerful mental concept that can easily derail our vision but when exactly our desire should be fulfilled is a question we ourselves may not know. We may think a certain desire should happen at a certain time without knowing all the ramifications once the desire has manifested. With time we should be flexible and trust that our consciousness will fulfill our desire at a time when it is best for us.

Manifest in Stages

When manifesting we must always start from where we are in order to get to where we want to go. First we need to realize where we stand right now before we visualize where we want to be. From this point "zero" we manifest the reality we desire.

Being in the now and focusing on our current condition uncovers our inherent creative resources. If we attempt to jump ahead and ignore what is happening now, we forego the chance to recognize that what we desire may already be in existence.

There is a difference between manifesting and fantasizing. Whereas in the latter we do not engage our intent to manifest but merely dwell in dreams, in manifestation we assess our current situation realistically before we focus on our desires.

One problem we may encounter is that recognizing our current situation may cause us to struggle to create a realistic vision for our future. This happens if the vision is too far from what we have experienced in our lives.

For example if up to now we have lived a middle class life and now we desire to be very rich, it may simply be impossible for us create a clear and realistic vision. We may not know how it feels to be very rich. To get around this dilemma we manifest in stages.

First we eliminate our fear of survival and poverty. This we accomplish by practicing non-resistance to our fear. Once our fear subsides we visualize that we are financially secure. As a result our creative energy grows and can handle larger visions. We then envision to be independently wealthy and eventually arrive at a vision of realistic wealth. Only realistic visions allow our awareness to rest upon them and prevent our subconscious from being engaged in a counter productive way.

On the level of feeling, the grander our vision the more expanded we feel. We manifest in several stages of expansion. First we visualize what is closest to us. As our creative energy expands so will our ability to envision realities on a larger scale.

Manifesting is not magic. Our desires will be fulfilled the same way all things come about in this world. Instead of visualizing that money will rain from the sky, or that we will win the lottery, it is more effective to visualize a more realistic scenario. Using common sense in manifesting increases the odds.

The Source of our Desires

We should not be too specific about how exactly our desire shall come into existence. When we are non-resistant, our consciousness determines the path of creation that is best for us.

For example if we have the desire to be wealthy, we should focus our awareness on the feeling of being wealthy and leave out the details about how we will reach it. The reason is that we cannot know how exactly our desire should be manifested.

For example if we visualize that our wealth shall come from an inheritance from a specific aunt, we are overly specific. Let us assume we in fact inherit one million dollars from our aunt but our aunt has a two million dollar debt which we will have to pay in order to be able to accept the inheritance. It would have been wiser to leave it up to our consciousness to decide how exactly the money should come to us. In this example it might have been more beneficial had the money come from a business venture we may have neglected to think about. We should leave room for our consciousness to decide on the source and manner of creation.

Let us look at another example. Let's assume we have a business venture and we are ready to sign a multi million dollar deal. Here it is save to visualize that the source of our millions will be the multi million dollar deal as long as we leave room for the unknown. At the end of each visualization we should let go of our desire and our vision and ask our consciousness to give us whatever is best for us. Being in the state of surrender to the wisdom and power of our consciousness ensures that we will receive what we want in the at the time and in the manner that is best for us.

Attaching the source of our desired reality to our vision is a way of conditioning our vision. For example if we visualize that we are happy because we are sitting in a beautiful garden of flowers, we attach the source of our happiness, which is the garden of flowers, to our vision of being happy. This condition engages our subconscious. Our subconscious will say that we are happy because of the beautiful garden of flowers and infer that if we were not in the garden of flowers we would not be happy. Without realizing we diminish the power of our vision.

It is perfectly fine however to acknowledge and enjoy the beautiful garden while we focus on our vision of being happy, versus making it the source of our happiness. In this example we must detach our feeling of happiness from its source so that we can fully experience our happiness. When we visualize that we are happy without any conditions or reasons, we unleash our creative power to manifest happiness no matter what circumstances we are in.

Letting go of our Vision

Letting go of our vision is just as important as creating our vision. Once our vision stands and has triggered intense positive feelings, we must let go of it.

Hanging on to our vision for too long will cause our subconscious to solidify the non-existence of our desired reality.

If we have not yet reached sufficient intensity of feeling we can relax more and start fresh with our vision.

As long as there is still the duality of observer and observed in us our mind has fertile ground to object to what we are doing.

For example if we envision to be happy, as long as we are in the process of visualizing, we have not yet become one with our perception of our vision. We are not completely immersed. We are still in the duality of being the observer and of being the one observed. In the above example our awareness has to merge with our feeling of happiness. Once our awareness merges with our feeling and we cease to observe, we become one with our Self and we fully experience happiness. At this stage our mind has disengaged. When our mind withdraws it lays open our inherent feeling of happiness. This feeling has always been there in us and with the help of our vision we now bring it to the foreground and into the field of our awareness.

Vision is only the beginning in manifesting. As long as we actively hold on to our vision, we have not yet become one with it. Only when our awareness becomes one with our perception of our vision will we merge with our vision. At that stage our vision has become reality on the level of feeling.

Letting go of our vision does not mean we should let go of our experience of our vision. Experiences come and go naturally. However we must let go of our initial intent to manifest. As long as we hold on to our desire to manifest we are subconsciously focusing on the non-existence of what we desire. Therefore letting go is the most important part in manifesting.

The key to letting go of our intent is gratitude. Each time we reach the point of experiencing our vision we must express gratitude. By expressing gratitude we let go of our intent. Gratitude has the effect of acknowledging the existence of our experience. The effect is that we shift our subconscious focus away from the non-existence of what we desire onto its existence.

The Power of Gratitude

Expressing gratitude is the fast track to happiness and success. It is one of the most powerful states for a person to be on. With gratitude we perceive the world in a positive light. This empowers us to recognize opportunities to be even more happy and successful. There is no moral imperative for gratitude. It is for our own benefit.

What if we cannot feel grateful for anything in our lives ?

There are many things in our lives we can be grateful about. This chapter however focuses on causeless gratitude. Causeless gratitude is the most powerful form of gratitude. It exists independently of internal or external circumstances and because of that it is there and can be expressed any time. Causeless gratitude is an attitude.

Before we begin to practice causeless gratitude let us think of something we can be grateful for at this moment in our lives. This practice opens our channel for gratitude to emerge and to strengthen. Through practice our conditional gratitude will transform into causeless gratitude. Eventually we will not need a reason for our gratitude to unfold.

Gratitude has the effect on widening our perception to perceive more aspects of reality. Gratitude frees our limited perception. Gratitude shifts our perception to perceive more beneficial aspects of reality. Gratitude can transform a pessimist into an optimistic.

Without gratitude, our perception could not find any positive aspect in the object of our perception if our inherent patterns did not allow for a positive angle. When we have causeless gratitude our perception has the freedom to take on a wider and independent viewpoint.

We perceive reality free from fear, anxiety and suffering.

Gratitude prevents our mind to worry about the future. With gratitude we realize that there is nothing that has to be done or accomplished in order for us to feel secure and happy. Gratitude gets us into the present moment.

I used to feel anxious whenever I got bills in the mail. My anxiety was disproportional to the actual bill. It was one of my inherent subconscious patterns to worry about money. When I began practicing gratitude I started seeing positive aspects whenever I thought about having to pay my bills. My fear had moved into the background. Free from my fear I discovered ways to save on my bills. I had missed this all the years. Through gratitude I could let go of my fear driven perception. As my perception became more free it allowed me to find solutions.

Over time the practice of gratitude creates a new positive pattern in us. It empowers us to see situations from different angels and to find the solutions that are most beneficial to us.

When we are grateful for a spiritual experience we acknowledge the existence of the experience. This has the effect that we perceive the experience as real and it prevents our subconscious to focus on its non-existence. Gratitude in spiritual practice ensures that we flow continuously through spiritual experiences and states of consciousness without being pulled out by our mind.

Gratitude enables us to feel devotion, sacredness and compassion. When we experience causeless gratitude, everything we perceive appears special, interesting, fascination and sacred. It is a feeling of connectedness with everything. Connectedness is what we need to manifest happiness and success in our lives. With gratitude we perceive the wonder of creation. Gratitude brings us closer to the mystery of creation. Once we are close to this wonder we will understand what creation is all about. We need this understanding to become empowered creators of our own reality.

Manifest in Oneness

The stages of Oneness are an important aspect in manifesting. On the first level of oneness we experience oneness with our Self. At this stage our awareness merges with our act of observing.

For example when we are not in oneness with our Self, when we listen to a sound we are aware that we are listening to that sound. There is the listening and there is our awareness. Once our awareness merges with the act of listening we experience oneness with our Self. We completely experience the act of listening. Our awareness is no longer separate from the act. There is no duality.

This first level of oneness is required when we manifest internal realities. Internal realities are our feelings, emotions and our physical health. We must become one with our vision to fully experience it. When we become completely one with our vision the desired state becomes reality.

On the second level we experience oneness with other people. In my own experience oneness with other people happens automatically when I experience oneness with my Self. When we are one with our Self our perception widens in order to experience the connectedness with other people. In my experiences when I feel one with my Self everything I perceive feels new and fresh. The space surrounding me feels thick and tangible. At that point the people I see appear to be closer and a feeling of connectedness emerges. I perceive the space between me and the people as a field that connects all of us. The more visceral the space feels the more intense my feeling of connectedness is.

The more intense the experience of oneness with other people is, the more we feel compassion for other people. Compassion arises from our realization that we are all made of the same essence. We are all connected with each other through this essence.

When we manifest good relationships and wealth we must feel connected with other people. Wealth usually comes to us from other people. Wealth flows from person to person. The person who is open and receptive will receive wealth. Oneness with other people empowers us to have positive and beneficial relationships that create opportunities to receive what we desire.

Experiencing oneness with other people makes us realize the essence of the other person. We realize that we are of the same essence. Our realization of oneness with other people is experienced as love. It flows through all the people. It is the space that surrounds us.

When we realize a person's essence, we cause a positive and mutually beneficial relationship with the person. We cease to be guided by our own subconscious patterns and by our reactions to the subconscious patterns of the other person.

The external form of whatever we perceive is only a reflection of its essence. Our mind causes us to only perceive the form. Therefore we feel separate. When we realize that our own essence is one with all that is, we experience the state of oneness with all that is and we realize who we truly are.

As is true for all states of consciousness once we reach them we recognize that we do not have to reach them anymore. Rather we realize that we already are whatever we want to become. When we realize this truth we become self-realized. This is the principle of oneness.

Manifesting Internal Realities
Introduction

When we are angry we are powerless. We believe that our anger comes from a source outside of us over which we have limited control. This is because we have not yet realized the true source of our emotions.

In this chapter we look at how our feelings and emotions can serve us better. Our emotions are dependent on our individual patterns and they are triggered by external circumstances. When we realize that the cause for our emotions is inside of us we become free from the external circumstances.

We yearn to be free from anger, anxiety and stress but do not know how to get there. We are at the mercy of external circumstances because we believe they are the source of our happiness. We strive to change our external circumstances to find happiness.

Sometimes when our circumstances become too heavy to bear we realize that our feelings come from within and are independent of the outer circumstance.

Fore example some people who are imprisoned for live or have an incurable disease find the source of their happiness to be inside of them. These people have given up on their attempt to change their external circumstance.

There is a nothing wrong with anger, sadness and discontent as long as we are aware that we do not have to be the victim of these feelings. Feelings are temporary and they continuously change. They transform as soon as we recognize their true source. Feelings that are seen as negative will become positive. We realize that negative and positive feelings are two sides of the same coin. Sadness transforms into inner peace. When our perception shifts, what once felt like sadness transforms into inner peace and happiness in the light of our awareness.

When we practice to manifest internal feelings we prepare our consciousness to bring about the external reality that matches our feeling. For example as we will learn in a subsequent chapter before we manifest wealth we must manifest wealth consciousness.

A part of successful manifesting is that we have to rise to a level of consciousness at which we can hold and enjoy what we have manifested. For example a person may have created tremendous wealth but suffers from poverty consciousness. There are many people who have become wealthy that were driven by their fear of being stuck in poverty. They still carry the same fear around. They may be wealthy but they cannot enjoy their wealth.

By manifesting our states of consciousness first, we prepare ourselves to receive and hold what we desire to manifest. When we visualize a desire, we must do this from a place of abundance and not a state of scarcity.

Internal states such as happiness, joy, inner peace and love are the training ground in manifestation before we move to external realities. The fluid nature of our feelings and emotions allows us to manifest them with little effort.

In my experience when I visualize myself being happy I instantly feel happy. This works at times when there is no resistance in me and when my mind is still.

It is important to distinguish feelings and emotions. Emotions are mind interpreted feelings and as such imply a condition, justification, cause or judgment. Feelings on the other hand arise in our body and have no content.

Feelings such as love and inner peace arise when our mind withdraws. They are natural states that are felt when our mind withdraws. Feelings are reflected in our bodies. Our bodies are the vessels and conduits for our feelings. Some feelings are dense and are stuck in certain places in our body and may cause physical pain. With the power of our awareness we can make them unstuck and enable them to move through our body. Once our feelings move they become subtle and either dissipate or transform into different feelings. Feelings can trigger emotions. For example we may be happy or content (emotions) for feeling inner peace and love (feelings).

When our feelings become so subtle that we no longer physically feel them, they transform into states of consciousness. The feeling of love has the potential to expand beyond the boundaries of our body and can encompass vast spaces. Love is then no longer felt physically. It has been transformed into a state of consciousness.

On the other hand we may experience a state of consciousness and feel the state in our physical body as a sensation. For example we may be in the state of consciousness of love which also is expressed in our physical body as an intense bodily sensation in our heart area. When we are present, our body reflects our states of consciousness.

Sometimes our feelings and emotions are densely compressed in our body. They cannot move and we perceive them as pain or numbness. Our focused awareness causes the feelings to become unstuck and to move in our body.

The Happiness Formula

Formula: <u>Vision + intent + non-resistance = Happiness</u>

When we align our consciousness with its expression,
our consciousness manifests through us.

Our limited mind suppresses our inherent positive feelings. Before we visualize a particular feeling our mind must withdraw and enable us to become receptive.

When we are non-resistant, we naturally detach from our mind. We begin to open up and perceive our inherent feelings such as inner peace and love. These feelings arise whenever our mind withdraws. With our intent and with visualization we enforce this process.

From the state of non-resistance we visualize ourselves being peaceful, loving and happy. We picture ourselves embodying the quality that we wish to manifest. It is important to have a clear image of ourselves.

We must rest our awareness on our vision and give up our observer role. The key is to let go of our intent to be aware. After we have formed the intent to rest our awareness on our vision we must let go of the intent and passively experience whatever happens. Just as we are aware of a picture on our desk, we must have a vision of love that simply exists without any doing on our part.

When our awareness merges with our experience of our vision of love we notice an opening inside of us. Through that opening an intense feeling will arise. This feeling is the expressed consciousness that matches our vision of love . As a consequence our vision and our consciousness become aligned.

We first focus our awareness on the particular aspect of our consciousness that we want to manifest. Then we feel its expression in our physical bodies. When the state of consciousness is aligned with our experience we become love. We embody the quality of love and we become loving.

With the help of gratitude we will be able harveste the full benefits of our experience.

For example let's assume we practice to manifest happiness and we only manage to create a weak feeling of happiness. If this happens we should avoid attempting to push ourselves to experience more happiness. The wanting of more denies what we already have. Instead we should express gratitude for the little happiness we feel. Our gratitude will cause our weak feeling to become stronger. Gratitude enhances the force of our experience.

The art of manifesting requires a balancing of active and passive; of using our intent and of being non-resistant.

We must avoid to condition our vision. For example we should not envision that we are happy because we have a nice home. This condition will create the wrong perception in us. We would perceive our happiness to be dependent on having the nice home.

Conditioning our vision on our inner states however is not harmful. For example we can envision that we are happy because we have reached inner peace. What we are doing is we condition our happiness on our state of inner peace. Since inner peace is an inherent inner state it is permanent. It is always in us whether we experience it or not.

Happiness is an individual and relative emotional response to our internal absolute state of inner peace. Happiness is relative since it is conditioned and needs a reason whereas inner peace is nothing other than our expressed essence. It needs no reason to exist.

To illustrate this let's look at the following example. Two people are in a state of inner peace. One of them feels happy about being at peace while the other person feels content about it. The same inner state caused two different emotions. Even though on the level of consciousness both people are in the state of inner peace, on the level of their individual personality they have different emotional responses to the same state of consciousness. The reason for this lies in the fact that our emotional responses come from of our mental interpretation. Every person interprets experiences differently according to our individual history and patterns. Over time as our personality changes our emotional responses change as well.

Therefore when we manifest internal states it is most effective to focus on universal internal states such as inner peace, love and compassion. Whatever emotion will be triggered by these states depends on us.

The Happiness Formula
My Experience

To illustrate how the happiness exercise works let me share one of my own experiences.

One day I sat in meditation posture. I formed the intent to be loving.

I visualized a field of love around my physical heart area. At first I observed myself sitting in meditation position with an aura of love. I fully rested my awareness on this image. I slowly let go of observing myself. Almost instantly I felt love emerging from my heart area and expanding throughout my body. It was a warm and pleasant feeling.

I experienced the love expanding from my body outwardly. I did not use my mind to reinforce the experience. I was riding the feeling of love.

I visualized myself sinking into myself. I sank into an opening in myself. I did not have any particular image of me sinking. I simply formed the intent to sink into myself. I landed in a vastly expanded state of consciousness. When I got out of this state and back into my body, I felt peace that was so subtle that I felt I was without boundaries. I had no inside or outside. My peace filled everything in me and around me. A wave of compassion and connectedness with the people around me emerged. The experience lasted for half a day.

I noticed that the more I practice manifesting the less I have to envision my internal state. My intent is sufficient for the inner sate to express itself.

Our mere intent combined with complete non-resistance will manifest our desire.

The Happiness Formula Exercise

Find a comfortable place where you can fully relax and be free from outside distraction.

Seven minute Breathing Exercise
Lay down or sit comfortably.

Close your eyes or leave them half way open whatever feels more comfortable.

Become aware of your breath. Do not actively focus on your breath. Be aware that there is breathing inside of you.

Breathe passively. Let the breathing happen and feel the air flowing through your body. Feel your body how it is being touched by your breathing.

Allow your breath to become subtle.

Now become aware of yourself observing your breath. Be aware of your awareness.

Relax and sink deeper. Relax deeper and deeper.

♦ ♦ ♦

Deep Relaxation Exercise for five minutes

For 5 minutes do the deep relaxation exercise.

Relax your body.
Be aware of your body.

Shift your awareness to your feet.
Relax your feet.

Shift your awareness to your lower legs.
Relax your lower legs.

Shift your awareness to your upper legs.
Relax your upper legs.

Shift your awareness to your hips.
Relax your hips.

Shift your awareness to your lower back.
Relax your lower back.

Shift your awareness to your back.
Relax your back.

Shift your awareness to your shoulders.
Relax your shoulders.

Shift your awareness to your neck.
Relax your neck.

Shift your awareness to your upper arm.
Relax your upper arm.

Shift your awareness to your lower arm.

Relax your lower arm.

Shift your awareness to your hands.
Relax your hands.

Shift your awareness to your belly.
Relax your belly.

Shift your awareness to your chest.
Relax your chest.

Shift your awareness to your throat.
Relax your throat.

Shift your awareness to your lips.
Relax your lips.

Shift your awareness to your nose.
Relax your nose.

Shift your awareness to your eyes
Relax your eyes.

Shift your awareness to your skull.
Relax your skull.

Shift your awareness to the top of your head.
Relax the top of your head.

Inhale deeply.
Hold your breath for 30 seconds then exhale and relax your entire body.

Again inhale deeply.
Hold your breath for 30 seconds then exhale and relax your entire body.

Feel your entire body relaxed.

Feel gratitude for being relaxed. Enjoy the feeling of relaxation and the feeling of gratitude.

Sink deeper and deeper.

If you are sleepy that is fine. You can take a nap.

If you feel you cannot relax do not force it. Accept that you cannot relax. And if you cannot accept that you cannot relax do not worry simply accept whatever is happening inside of you.

Be non-resistant to whatever you feel.

Do not expect any particular result from this exercise.

Sink deeper and enjoy your state. Nobody is judging you.

Relax deeper.

♦ ♦ ♦

Look around the room. Notice any change in your perception.

Pick an internal state such as love, compassion, inner peace or joy. Visualize yourself embodying this quality.

Produce a clear and detailed image of yourself. Visualize yourself expressing the desired feeling.

For example you may see yourself with a big smile on our face or you can visualize how love is emanating from your heart area.

Once you have a clear vision, rest your awareness on that vision. Let go of creating the vision and simply rest on it. It is now time to be receptive to what you have created in your vision.

Passively experience the image with your awareness.

Be aware of your awareness and how it is resting on your vision.

Passively observe your vision as if it was a photo that you are looking at.

Then feel whatever feeling is in your body.

Do not push yourself into feeling or experiencing something. The feeling will emerge from an opening in your body that you have created with this exercise.

If you do not feel anything in the beginning that is perfectly natural. Simply enjoy the process and be grateful for doing this exercise. A feeling will eventually emerge.

Conclude the exercise.

Manifesting Physical Health
Introduction

The formula I use to manifest physical health is based on the principal that our body has its own intelligence. Instead of actively applying healing energy to our body, we access the affected area in our body and allow the body to use its own resources to remedy the pain.

Our body's natural state is being healthy. Pain and disease are caused when our own inherent energies cannot flow in our body. Dense energies are blockages in our bodies and are experienced as pain. The source of these dense areas are past experiences and physical ailments caused by external factors.

The goal is to become non-resistant in our physical and mental bodies. In the state of non-resistance our energies can flow. At this stage we will form the intent to be healthy and the health aspect of our consciousness causes our own healing energies to do the work.

The healing formula is based on the principle of oneness with our Self. Most of the times there is little or no awareness in our body. Many bodily functions occur without our awareness. When we direct our awareness to the affected area in our body, it causes an opening in our body. Through that opening our healing resources emerge. When we access our body intelligence with our awareness, our body begins to send signals to our mind about the source of the ailment. Our focused awareness causes us to receive intuitive insights about what needs to be done to heal ourselves and about the cause of the physical problem.

Healing ourselves is a gradual process and we may need to use other remedies and traditional medicine as well. When we practice healing ourselves with our own healing energies we increase the positive effects of traditional medicine.

The Healing Formula

Formula: <u>Physical Pain + Awareness = Body Intelligence + Healing</u>

When we are non-resistant to our pain our focused
awareness frees up our body intelligence to heal itself.

We access our body intelligence by directing our awareness onto the area of the pain. To help focus our awareness onto the affected area we can put our hand on or close to the pain area. Our awareness becomes one with the area in our body. Our mind ceases to resist the pain. By resisting, our mind solidifies the existence of the pain further. We allow the pain to be. In non-resistance we gain strength that is otherwise used up by our resistance.

When our awareness is focused on our pain, the affected area opens up. The pain starts to move and it becomes less dense.

Our awareness helps the area to free up our body intelligence. Our body begins to send information to our mind. We use our mind to interpret the signal to find out about the cause of the pain. Often our body naturally adjusts a certain posture or relaxes a certain muscle when we put our awareness on the area of the pain. By observing how our body adjusts we learn from it.

When I wrote this book I sat for long hours typing on my computer. I would feel pain in my back. I focused my awareness on the area in the back where the pain was located. I fully felt the pain and allowed it to be without resisting. My back would start making certain movements to the left and right to adjust itself and the pain disappeared.

Once we realize that our body has the wisdom to heal itself, it will start to do so. By giving up resistance to what is happening in the present moment we free up our physical resources to heal our body. When we are able to accept our pain, we are in the right state of mind to visualize ourselves being healthy.

Focused awareness merges with our body consciousness. Information from the body then reaches our mind. Our mind will interpret and use the information to find the right remedy.

The Healing Formula Exercise

Seven minute Breathing Exercise
Lay down or sit comfortably.

Close your eyes or leave them half way open whatever feels more comfortable.

Become aware of your breath. Do not actively focus on your breath. Be aware that there is breathing inside of you.

Breathe passively. Let the breathing happen and feel the air flowing through your body. Feel your body how it is being touched by your breathing.

Allow your breath to become subtle.

Now become aware of yourself observing your breath. Be aware of your awareness.

Relax and sink deeper. Relax deeper and deeper.

♦　♦　♦

Deep Relaxation Exercise for five minutes

For 5 minutes do the deep relaxation exercise.

Relax your body.
Be aware of your body.

Shift your awareness to your feet.
Relax your feet.

Shift your awareness to your lower legs.
Relax your lower legs.

Shift your awareness to your upper legs.
Relax your upper legs.

Shift your awareness to your hips.
Relax your hips.

Shift your awareness to your lower back.
Relax your lower back.

Shift your awareness to your back.
Relax your back.

Shift your awareness to your shoulders.
Relax your shoulders.

Shift your awareness to your neck.
Relax your neck.

Shift your awareness to your upper arm.
Relax your upper arm.

Shift your awareness to your lower arm.
Relax your lower arm.

Shift your awareness to your hands.
Relax your hands.

Shift your awareness to your belly.
Relax your belly.

Shift your awareness to your chest.
Relax your chest.

Shift your awareness to your throat.
Relax your throat.

Shift your awareness to your lips.
Relax your lips.

Shift your awareness to your nose.
Relax your nose.

Shift your awareness to your eyes
Relax your eyes.

Shift your awareness to your skull.
Relax your skull.

Shift your awareness to the top of your head.
Relax the top of your head.

Inhale deeply.
Hold your breath for 30 seconds then exhale and relax your entire body.

Again inhale deeply.
Hold your breath for 30 seconds then exhale and relax your entire body.

Feel your entire body relaxed.

Feel gratitude for being relaxed. Enjoy the feeling of relaxation and the feeling of gratitude.

Sink deeper and deeper.

If you are sleepy that is fine. You can take a nap.

If you feel you cannot relax do not force it. Accept that you cannot relax. And if you cannot accept that you cannot relax do not worry simply accept whatever is happening inside of you.

Be non-resistant to whatever you feel.

Do not expect any particular result from this exercise.

Sink deeper and enjoy your state. Nobody is judging you.

Relax deeper.

◆　◆　◆

Now focus on a pain or any uncomfortable feeling in your body.

If you do not have any ache or pain you can focus on a positive feeling you wish to manifest in your body and on the area where you want to feel it.

Visualize yourself. See a clear image of yourself with the particular positive feeling. If you have a pain in your body, allow yourself to feel the pain. Let go of resistance and let the pain move freely in your body. Then start the visualization.

Remember that as with all visualizations you want to start from where you are and acknowledge the current situation and go from there.

Focus your awareness on the vision and completely experience whatever feeling emerges from the vision. If nothing happens do not resist. Be grateful for whatever is in the present moment. Your gratitude will shift you into a feeling and allow your mind to withdraw.

Now focus on the area where the pain is located. Ask your body "what is the matter about this pain" ? and "how it can this pain go away".

Now let go of any expectation. Fully relax and accept whatever is at the present moment. If an intuitive thought about this pain arises, make a note of it. If your body makes certain movements it may be that it is accessing its own wisdom to alleviate the pain.

If you feel any change take a note. Conclude the exercise.

Manifesting Beyond Our Physical Boundaries
Introduction

When we experience how we are connected with other people we are able to manifest the relationships we want in our lives.

Instead of manifesting in an isolated space, we must realize that we are connected with all people. There is something between us and the people around us that connects us all. We will use this realization to manifest good relationships for us.

With the help of non-resistance, reduced mind activity and presence, our awareness can merge with our perception. Imagine you are sitting on your desk and you are looking at a picture on the wall. Instead of observing yourself looking at the picture and thinking about yourself looking at the picture you experience the act of looking at the picture. You stop thinking of yourself as the observer and you only experience your act of looking.

Oneness with our Self is the stepping stone to oneness with other people. Imagine you were fully immersed in looking at the picture and a person enters the room. You will naturally feel connected to the essence of that person. Feeling one with other people causes us to deeply understand the essence of the other person and to feel compassion for that person.

When we are one with the act, there is no mind activity. Our sensory perception changes. In my own experiences the objects I looked at appeared to move closer to me. They become more clear and crisp. I feel I can experience the essence of what I perceive. The object felt as if it was alive. I remember after a deep meditation I sat in a chair and looked at the white wall of the living room. The wall felt alive. I was fascinated and in awe by the aliveness and the mystery of that wall. I had experienced oneness with my act of looking and one with the object of my perception.

We are not one with the external form of what we perceive but with its essence. We recognize that we are one with this essence because we are made of this essence. When we experience this essence we feel deeply connected to all people.

To illustrate the meaning of the "essence" let us the example of the ocean. All people and things are like waves in the ocean. On the surface each wave appears to be separate from the other waves however all the waves are connected with each other by the ocean. Our essence is the water. It is the same water in all the waves. Looking upwards from below, the waves are indistinguishable. Only on the surface do they appear to be separate. They are the different aspects of the same ocean.

In my own experience whenever I am in the state of oneness, my interactions with the people become more direct and immediate as if something in me already knew what the other person would say or do. There is a natural flow between myself and the other person.

It is our natural state to be connected to all people. Once the filter of our mind has been lifted we will experience people in a new light. We will perceive people in a more direct and instant way.

This state of consciousness is an important step to manifest good relationships. Good relationships do not fall from the sky but require the free flow of knowledge and realization of our common essence.

The Power of the Space

To describe what I mean by the Space let me refer to my own experience.

When I feel the space I feel connected with the essence of the people and things around me. Sometimes I perceive the space as an entity in itself and at other times I perceive it as the essence that is in me and in all people and things. I feel held by it. It feels as if the space has its own intelligence.

When I experience the Space my actions appear to be automatic. The Space feels visceral.

Just as the waves in the ocean are the visible tips of the body of water, I felt like the people around me were the visible parts of the space. It felt like all my actions, my body movements, me talking and looking were all happening within this Space. It felt that whatever happened in the space was reflected in the people around me. As if the Space was reflecting itself onto the people. It seemed as if the Space was the true intelligence and the people were its reflections.

In the presence of this Space our thoughts are powerful, people react positively and everything falls into place. In this state I feel one with all the people yet detached from their external form. I experience my own essence as one with the essence of all the people.

The people's forms are the individualized expressions of the essence. The individualized form is made of the peoples patterns, thoughts and history. On the level of the Space the peoples judgments and thoughts could not affect me. There was no "me" for their judgments to attach to. It is not that I was mindless. I was thinking but I was detached from my thoughts. My thoughts did not affect my experience.

Being detached from peoples thoughts, judgments and projections yet connected to their true essence is pure joy. Our own actions arise out of our inherent states of joy, love and peace. We cease to look for our happiness in other people.

The Space and the essence of all people and things are one and the same. However at times we may experience the Space as an independent field that surrounds us and at other times we feel it as being the essence that is in us, surrounds us and is in everything that is. On the level of oneness they are one and the same.

The Power of Perception

In order to manifest good relationships we must understand how we relate to other people. We accomplish this by understanding how our perception works.

In the first book we examined how to become free from our limited perception. In this chapter we will revisit this principle as it relates to manifesting.

Everything we perceive with our senses is relative to ourselves. Whatever we perceive is being colored by our own views, patterns, experiences, upbringings and personal history. Perception is dependent on the perceiver. Whatever we perceive exists only in our perception.

For example one person looking at a tree may perceive the tree as a beautiful plant whereas another person looking at the same tree may see an object that blocks his view. Neither of the two people are able to really see what is there; simply a tree.

We are prisoners of our limited perception. When we understand how our perception works we can become free from its limitations. When we are aware of our act of perceiving we realize our perception is controlled by our mind. For example we may have a particular perception about a person we know. If the person changes, our perception remains. Our perception of this person was formed by our past experiences with that person. We believe we perceive the reality of this person. When our perception becomes more flexible, we realize that our perception is shaped by our own individual viewpoints. Our image of the person is relative and dependent on us. The key is to be aware that what we see is not the person itself but a product of our perception.

The first step in gaining an open perception is to realize that our perception is limited. The second step is to let go of our resistance to our limited perception. We cannot change our limited perception with our mind, so we must accept it. Once we fully surrender to our limited perception, it will loosen and become fluid. When we become relaxed, nonjudgmental and open, our perception will become flexible. We are the reference point for our perception.

Once our perception is fluid it will move and transform into a wider perception. The new perception will be free from our prejudices. We begin to see things in a new light. We perceive more aspects of the same reality. The more aspects we can perceive the more opportunities we have.

With practice we will be able to create a pattern of perceiving everything from the most positive and beneficial viewpoint.

Our perception is often rigid, dense and stuck in a certain pattern. Once we focus our awareness onto it, its limits begin to move and eventually dissipate.

Our perception becomes objective when it is not solely based on our individual patterns but is based on something that is common to all people. The perception that is based on our common essence is always beneficial to us and it will never hurt other people. The perception that is based on fear or greed cannot benefit us. A negative and limited perception will eventually catch up with us. It will create the realities in our lives on which it is based.

The key is to be aware of what it is that controls our perception. When we do not resist what controls our perception it will lose its power.

Once our perception is free, it will take on different viewpoints of the same reality. The more angels of reality we can perceive, the more objective our vision becomes. The more objective our vision becomes the better we understand reality. The better we understand reality, the wiser we become. The wiser we become, the more powerful our manifestations will be.

The Relationship Formula
Introduction

Everybody needs good Relationships to enjoy live. To manifest what we desire, we need good relationships with other people. We cannot manifest joy, happiness and wealth out of thin air. We need good relationships with people who will help us in getting what we desire.

Joyful and beneficial relationships are based on clarity. Clarity in our relationships fosters the free flow of energy and information. The less our relationships are based on our own individual patterns and the more they arise out of the understanding of our common essence, the more harmonious, joyful and beneficial they become.

Clarity in relationships allows for energy and information to flow between people Relationships that are based only on our individual patterns and viewpoints have no common ground. Under this scenario there will be two people with two relationships. Both parties to the relationship only experience the relationship through their own limited perception.

We should not settle with mediocre relationships. When we focus on our essence as the common denominator for our relationships, all our relationships will become good and mutually beneficial. Mutually beneficial relationships foster joy and prosperity.

Manifesting good Relationships with our Self

Formula: <u>Balance (Body + Mind + Consciousness) = Good Relationship</u>

When all the aspects of our Self are in balance with each other we have a good relationship with ourselves.

Every relationship starts with ourselves. Before we focus on our relationships with others we must set right our relationship with ourselves.

We all have felt that our body wants one thing and our mind wants a another thing. We abuse our body with excessive eating and drinking because we are stressed and anxious. The problem is that we have an unhealthy and imbalanced relationship between our different aspects of our Self. By setting right our relationship with our Self, we bring our different aspects of our Self in harmony with each other. For it to work we must understand the relationship between our different aspects in ourselves.

With the help of our awareness we are able to bring all the aspects of our Self in harmony with each other. We begin to understand how they affect each other. By listening and focusing our awareness on our different aspects we learn about ourselves.

For example in the previous chapter I talked about how we can learn from our body by listening to its own body intelligence. We saw how our emotions emerge from our sensory feelings and how they are interpreted by our mind. We learned how our perception is dependent on our mind and how it can become free from it. When we practice awareness we gain insight into the different aspects of our Self.

When we have good relationships with all the parts of our Self, we gain vitality and wisdom. Our actions will naturally benefit us. We gain clarity about what we want in life. We become clear about our desires. We balance the needs of our different aspects to benefit us as a whole.

Practicing non-resistance to the relationship we have with ourselves, fosters positive change. We must be non-judgmental with ourselves. Judging ourselves is not harmful as long as we accept the fact that we are judging ourselves. However judging ourselves for judging ourselves causes a vicious cycle of thoughts and afterthoughts.

When we experience the essence of our Self we have the best possible relationship with our self.

When we have clarity about the needs of our different aspects of our Self, we gain clarity about what we want in our relationships with others. The other person will sense our clarity and either match it or avoid us. There will be no ambiguity and contradiction in the signals we send out to the other person.

Manifesting good Relationships with Others

Formula: <u>Clarity + Awareness of the Essence in others = Good Relationship</u>

When we realize that we are all made of the same essence we gain clarity of what we want from our relationships. We will manifest the relationships we want in our lives.

There are as many relationships as there are people in a relationship.

Due to our limited perception we can only experience our relationship with another person from our own viewpoint. The same is true for the other person. On the level of form there is no universal ground for relationships.

Granted there are common societal and moral guidelines and values that apply to relationships. However before we experience the essence of those moral guidelines and values we follow them blindly and they do not bring us closer to each other.

Truly beneficial relationships have the quality of freedom and non-judgment. They go beyond the individual personalities of the people in them. They are based on the common essence of the people. It is the nature of our essence to connect itself with itself by connecting us with other people.

To illustrate how relative our relationships are on the level of form let's look at romantic relationships. Romantic relationships consist of unconditional and conditional love, physical, emotional and mental attraction, affection, enthusiasm, longing, attachment, pain of separation, expectation, disappointment, anger, hatred and so on. Some of these aspects we would not recognize as love at all. Usually the pleasant aspects of love are dominant in the beginning whereas the unpleasant aspects arise in later stages of the relationship.

In some relationships we experience only pleasant aspects. One reason may be that there simply are no circumstances that would trigger any unpleasant aspects. Or the reason may be that the pleasant aspects of the relationship are so strong that they dominate the entire relationship.

How do we consciously create such positive, uplifting and mutually beneficial relationships ?

Instead of trying to figure out all the personality traits of a person and match them with our own personality, we should focus on that what forms the basis of good relationships. The basis is our common essence. When we are aware of our common essence we will not enter into a relationship looking to obtain love. We will enter any relationship to express and expand the love we already have inside.

There is nothing wrong with figuring out another person's personality and matching it with one's own personality and life circumstances as long as we are aware that this has nothing to do with love.

When we are one with other people we perceive their essence despite their different personality and life circumstances. On the level of oneness we enter into a relationship in complete freedom and non-attachment to the circumstances of the relationship and to particular attributes of the other person. Once we recognize the underlying essence of all relationships we realize the common relationship that exists between us.

We often believe that we entered into a relationship because of love. However there are many other reason for entering into a relationship. There is our need to feel loved and there may be financial reasons or the fear of being alone and so on. As long as there is a need for a relationship, our mind will attach conditions, judgments and concepts to the relationship. This prevents the relationship to find its common essence and as such it is doomed to miss its highest potential.

On the level of oneness all relationships are based on the expression of unconditional love. All relationships are based on this principle. When we realize this, our relationships become wonderful.

At this stage we continue to experience the love in our relationships in all its different expressions but they will no longer dominate our well being. We will be aware of them without being affected. We will recognize that all the expressions of the essence through a person are the individualized expression of the one all encompassing love that flows through all people.

Our relationships become light, free and secure. We realize that we are not dependent on getting love from another person. We feel love as an expansion of our own essence. When we are secure and sure of our own love, we can be very practical about our relationships.

There is no need to be attached to a particular expression of love. Expressions in this physical world change. When we experience that the essence of all people never changes we are free to let go of our attachment to a certain kind of expression of love.

We begin to manifest all our relationships harmoniously and in a beneficial manner. We are clear about our motivation for entering into a relationship.

When we have dropped our need for love we become more practical about the reasons to enter into a relationship. When we realize the essence of all relationships, we begin to enter relationships from a place of freedom and non-attachment. This does not mean that we will no longer enjoy the varies expressions of the essence in form. To the contrary since we do not have the fear of losing love, we will enjoy its expressions more intensely.

When we realize that we will never end up without love, we will feel secure in our relationships. We will be free and we will be able to focus on the practical and joyful aspects of the relationship. We are able to communicate our intentions and expectations clearly to the other person. When we communicate with the other person, the other person will intuitively grasp the meaning of what we say. Realizing that everything in the physical world changes, we become more light hearted, forgiving and loving in our relationships.

When we are non-resistant and accepting of our relationships, our perception becomes aware of the positive aspects of our relationships. We perceive our relationships more objectively. Our enhanced perception reveals new viewpoints that empower us to benefit from and grasp the opportunities in our relationships.

Manifesting Good Relationships with Our Self Exercise

The goal of this exercise is to get to know our Self. We want to become aware of our needs and our strengths in order to bring all the parts of our Self in harmony. When we are in harmony with our Self, we are naturally happy and we will know what we truly want.

In this exercise we will chose one area of our Self to focus our awareness on.

Seven minute Breathing Exercise
Lay down or sit comfortably.

Close your eyes or leave them half way open whatever feels more comfortable.

Become aware of your breath. Do not actively focus on your breath. Be aware that there is breathing inside of you.

Breathe passively. Let the breathing happen and feel the air flowing through your body. Feel your body how it is being touched by your breathing.

Allow your breath to become subtle.

Now become aware of yourself observing your breath. Be aware of your awareness.

Relax and sink deeper. Relax deeper and deeper.

♦ ♦ ♦

Deep Relaxation Exercise for five minutes
For 5 minutes do the deep relaxation exercise.

Relax your body.
Be aware of your body.

Shift your awareness to your feet.
Relax your feet.

Shift your awareness to your lower legs.
Relax your lower legs.

Shift your awareness to your upper legs.
Relax your upper legs.

Shift your awareness to your hips.
Relax your hips.

Shift your awareness to your lower back.
Relax your lower back.

Shift your awareness to your back
Relax your back.

Shift your awareness to your shoulders.
Relax your shoulders.

Shift your awareness to your neck.
Relax your neck.

Shift your awareness to your upper arm.
Relax your upper arm.

Shift your awareness to your lower arm.
Relax your lower arm.

Shift your awareness to your hands.
Relax your hands.

Shift your awareness to your belly.
Relax your belly.

Shift your awareness to your chest.
Relax your chest.

Shift your awareness to your throat.
Relax your throat.

Shift your awareness to your lips
Relax your lips.

Shift your awareness to your nose.
Relax your nose.

Shift your awareness to your eyes
Relax your eyes.

Shift your awareness to your skull.
Relax your skull.

Shift your awareness to the top of your head.
Relax the top of your head.

Inhale deeply.
Hold your breath for 30 seconds then exhale and relax your entire body.

Again inhale deeply.
Hold your breath for 30 seconds then exhale and relax your entire body.

Feel your entire body relaxed.

Feel gratitude for being relaxed. Enjoy the feeling of relaxation and the feeling of gratitude.

Sink deeper and deeper.

If you are sleepy that is fine. You can take a nap.

If you feel you cannot relax do not force it. Accept that you cannot relax. And if you cannot accept that you cannot relax, do not worry, simply accept whatever is happening inside of you.

Be non-resistant to whatever you feel.

Do not expect any particular result from this exercise.

Sink deeper and enjoy your state. Nobody is judging you.

Relax deeper.

◆ ◆ ◆

Now pick an area of yourself that has been bothering you.

For example you can pick a physical issue such as you may suffer from excessive food craving or from addiction. Or you can chose an issue that involves your mind. For example you may have anxiety or excessive thoughts. Or excessive day dreaming or uncontrollable negative thoughts and emotions.

Once you have picked and located the area in your body, stay with it. Allow this particular issue to be as it is. Practice non-resistance to it. If you see yourself unable to let go of resistance then allow this resistance. This is a for of non-resistance too.

Practice gratitude that you have located the problem inside of you and you are feeling something.

Instead of mentally analyzing the problem, rest your awareness on it.

Be aware of the fact that you have an individually colored perception of this particular problem. Allow your perception to be. Do not resist it. If you do not like your perception and you cannot give up your resistance then do not give up your resistance. Instead give up your wanting of giving it up.

Relax deeper and deeper. Allow your perception to relax. Stay with whatever is and be grateful. Your feeling of gratitude will open your perception. Do not hold on to any experience you may have. Let your experiences come and go freely. Be ready for the new experience to arise.

Be grateful for feeling a widening of your perception. You are becoming detached from your perception.

If you have an inspirational thought or a feeling of joy, love or inner peace stay with it.

You may gain a new and wider perception and valuable information about your problem.

For example your body may reveal the true cause of the problem.

Your perception may alter. You may receive an inspiration as to what the problem is truly about and what you can do to remedy it.

Your mind may now understand your problem deeper. For example an excessive craving may be your need for love and security. These kinds of insights arise once you allow yourself to be immersed in the awareness of the problem without having a predetermined judgment about it.

Conclude the exercise.

Manifesting Good Relationships with Others Exercise I

Seven minute Breathing Exercise
Lay down or sit comfortably.

Close your eyes or leave them half way open whatever feels more comfortable.

Become aware of your breath. Do not actively focus on your breath. Be aware that there is breathing inside of you.

Breathe passively. Let the breathing happen and feel the air flowing through your body. Feel your body how it is being touched by your breathing.

Allow your breath to become subtle.

Now become aware of yourself observing your breath. Be aware of your awareness.

Relax and sink deeper. Relax deeper and deeper.

♦ ♦ ♦

Deep Relaxation Exercise for five minutes
For 5 minutes do the deep relaxation exercise.

Relax your body.
Be aware of your body.

Shift your awareness to your feet.
Relax your feet.

Shift your awareness to your lower legs.
Relax your lower legs.

Shift your awareness to your upper legs.
Relax your upper legs.

Shift your awareness to your hips.
Relax your hips.

Shift your awareness to your lower back.
Relax your lower back.

Shift your awareness to your back.
Relax your back.

Shift your awareness to your shoulders.
Relax your shoulders.

Shift your awareness to your neck.
Relax your neck.

Shift your awareness to your upper arm.
Relax your upper arm.

Shift your awareness to your lower arm.
Relax your lower arm.

Shift your awareness to your hands.
Relax your hands.

Shift your awareness to your belly.
Relax your belly.

Shift your awareness to your chest.
Relax your chest.

Shift your awareness to your throat.
Relax your throat.

Shift your awareness to your lips
Relax your lips.

Shift your awareness to your nose.
Relax your nose.

Shift your awareness to your eyes.
Relax your eyes.

Shift your awareness to your skull.
Relax your skull.

Shift your awareness to the top of your head.
Relax the top of your head.

Inhale deeply.
Hold your breath for 30 seconds then exhale and relax your entire body.

Again inhale deeply.
Hold your breath for 30 seconds then exhale and relax your entire body.

Feel your entire body relaxed.

Feel gratitude for being relaxed. Enjoy the feeling of relaxation and the feeling of gratitude.

Sink deeper and deeper.

If you are sleepy that is fine. You can take a nap.

If you feel that you cannot relax do not force it. Accept that you cannot relax. And if you cannot accept that you cannot relax, do not worry, simply accept whatever is happening inside of you.

Be non-resistant to whatever you feel.

Do not expect any particular result from this exercise.

Sink deeper and enjoy your state. Nobody is judging you.

Relax deeper.

◆ ◆ ◆

Now pick a relationship with another person.

Put your awareness on this relationship.

Observe any feeling that may come up when you think about this relationship.

If there are unpleasant or pleasant feelings welcome those feelings in your body.

Do no resist your feelings or thoughts about this relationship.

Be grateful that you are feeling something.

If there is an unpleasant feeling do not be judgmental. If you are compelled to judge then feel free to judge and give up judging yourself for judging.

If it is a pleasant feeling enjoy it but do not hold on to it. Express gratitude.

Sink deeper.

Ask yourself: "what is hidden underneath the feelings I have" ?

"What is the cause for the unpleasant or the pleasant feelings" ?

Do not expect an answer right away simply relax deeper into yourself.

If a clear thought arises it may be an answer to your question. Take note of it.

Your current feeling may change due to the fact that your awareness is shining its light on it. You may feel it now in a different area of your body. It may become stronger or weaker.

Become aware of your perception of this relationship.

Allow this perception to be and do not resist it. Be grateful for being aware of your perception.

Your perception may shift at this point. A new perception may emerge. Enjoy the new perception without holding on to it.

You may see a different detail of the relationship or you may experience a different perception of the same problem that you have in this relationship.

If you get an insight make a note about it for later use. If your perception or feeling changed note this down as well.

Complete the exercise with a deep feeling of gratitude.

Conclude the exercise.

Manifesting Good Relationships with Others Exercise II

Where in Exercise One you uncovered the problems, the goal of this exercise is to use visualization to manifest good relationships.

Chose the same relationship as in the previous exercise.

Seven minute Breathing Exercise
Lay down or sit comfortably.

Close your eyes or leave them half open whatever feels more comfortable.

Become aware of your breath. Do not actively focus on your breath. Be aware that there is breathing inside of you.

Breathe passively. Let the breathing happen and feel the air flowing through your body. Feel your body how it is being touched by your breathing.

Allow your breath to become subtle.

Now become aware of yourself observing your breath. Be aware of your awareness.

Relax and sink deeper. Relax deeper and deeper.

◆ ◆ ◆

Deep Relaxation Exercise for five minutes
For 5 minutes do the deep relaxation exercise.

Relax your body.
Be aware of your body.

Shift your awareness to your feet.
Relax your feet.

Shift your awareness to your lower legs.
Relax your lower legs.

Shift your awareness to your upper legs.
Relax your upper legs.

Shift your awareness to your hips.
Relax your hips.

Shift your awareness to your lower back.
Relax your lower back.

Shift your awareness to your back.
Relax your back.

Shift your awareness to your shoulders.
Relax your shoulders.

Shift your awareness to your neck.
Relax your neck.

Shift your awareness to your upper arm.
Relax your upper arm.

Shift your awareness to your lower arm.
Relax your lower arm.

Shift your awareness to your hands.
Relax your hands.

Shift your awareness to your belly.
Relax your belly.

Shift your awareness to your chest.
Relax your chest.

Shift your awareness to your throat.
Relax your throat.

Shift your awareness to your lips
Relax your lips.

Shift your awareness to your nose.
Relax your nose.

Shift your awareness to your eyes
Relax your eyes.

Shift your awareness to your skull.
Relax your skull.

Shift your awareness to the top of your head.
Relax the top of your head.

Inhale deeply.
Hold your breath for 30 seconds then exhale and relax your entire body.

Again inhale deeply.
Hold your breath for 30 seconds then exhale and relax your entire body.

Feel your entire body relaxed.

Feel gratitude for being relaxed. Enjoy the feeling of relaxation and the feeling of gratitude.

Sink deeper and deeper.

If you are sleepy that is fine. You can take a nap.

If you feel you cannot relax do not force it. Accept that you cannot relax. And if you cannot accept that you cannot relax, do not worry, simply accept whatever is happening inside of you.

Be non-resistant to whatever you feel.

Do not expect any particular result from this exercise.

Sink deeper and enjoy your state. Nobody is judging you.

Relax deeper.

♦ ♦ ♦

Now visualize your relationship with that person.

Visualize how you want your relationship to be. Get a clear and detailed image of you and the other person with this good relationship.

Do not push or artificially create a positive image. Simply see yourself and the other person.

When you are relaxed and you feel comfortable with yourself, allow all negative feelings to be. Then allow them to move and become lighter and dissipate. Become an empty bowl.

If are fully relaxed, feel how the negative feeling starts moving and how it may leave your body and may morph into a different feeling.

When you feel like an empty bowl with no particular feeling toward the other person you are ready to include the other person into your vision. You may project the new feeling that has emerged in you onto this relationship.

Express gratitude for feeling this new feeling in connection with this relationship.

If there are deeply ingrained negative feelings towards this relationship then first chose a different relationship so you can gain the experience of uncovering and moving the negative feelings, before you take on your most difficult relationships.

If you feel a new positive feeling and you have included the other person into the vision, ask how this relationship may remain this positive for the long term.

Relax deeper. Do not expect an answer. An intuitive thought may arise at a later time and provide you with a sudden clear answer.

You may suddenly see the negative issue in this relationship from a positive viewpoint. You may also realize a shift in your perception.

You may receive an insight about a particular opportunity to make this relationship better.

These insights mostly arise when you least expect them. They arise when your mind is open and receptive.

Write down any insights you may have gained in this exercise.

Conclude the exercise.

The Wealth Formula
Introduction

Manifest to obtain what you love not to escape from what we do not love.

To manifest wealth there must be clarity of vision and clarity of motivation. We must determine what exactly we want and we must have clarity about why we want it.

We need to be clear about the details of our vision and we must know our true motivation for our desire. When both requirements are met our vision is powerful.

In addition to having a clear image we must envision the feeling we have when our desire has become reality. Both vision and feeling it must be a present moment experience. When our vision is clear and detailed, our awareness is strong and focused. Our awareness treats our vision as reality. Think for a moment that you are looking at a blurry image of something that is far away. Your perception of the image would be spotty and your mind would attempt to fill in the gaps in your vision. If the image is too incomplete you would not recognize it as real. The same is true when you create your internal image. If the image is clear, your mind won't be needed to fill in the gaps. With nothing left to do for the mind, it will withdraw. If on the other hand the mind is needed to complete an incomplete image our subconscious will reinforce its non-existence.

Most people desire wealth because of fear of poverty. We believe what we want is wealth but we disregard the real problem.

The fear is real. Even the rich are full of fear. However our efforts to manifest and enjoy wealth when we are motivated by fear are doomed to fail. While it is possible to create wealth based on fear, many rich people in fact have done it, it is impossible to enjoy our wealth without eliminating our fear. Fear of survival will not go away when we are wealthy.

I can speak from my own experience. At one time I had rapid growth and profits in my law firm. However I could never get rid of my feeling of financial insecurity.

The longer we are wealthy and enjoy relative security, our insecurity and anxiety may disappear on the surface, but it remains dormant in our mind. External wealth cannot substitute inner peace. A wealthy person knows he/she can lose everything. A sudden illness, law suit, divorce, market crash and so on can take away any assumed external security. Only the person who is detached from the need to find security through wealth will be able to fully enjoy wealth.

We must acknowledge our fear, feel it, not resist it and let it go. Even if the fear goes away only for a moment, it will be sufficient for our positive energies to arise from within us. We do not need to eradicate our fear. All that is required is that we are aware of it. Awareness of our fear diminishes the effect it has on us.

When we are aware of our fear, we must stay with it. Instead of thinking about the content of our fear we allow it to exist as a physical feeling in our body. Our awareness will loosen the grip of the fear on our body.

Once the fear has dissipated, we are ready to visualize being wealthy and focus to on the positive feelings wealth can cause.

We may discover that after our fear has gone our desire disappears too. For example lets assume we have the desire to be free from lack of money and to be a powerful business person who owns a company with many employees. Once our fear of lack of money has vanished we may no longer feel the desire to have a big business either. Instead we may discover our true passion. If however we ignore our fear, we run the risk that it will make us do thinks that harm us. In the previous example, had we been focused on the big business in order to escape our financial fear, we may have missed details in connection with our desire for the big business that we do not want. Having a big businesses can cause big stress and fear of losing it, aspects we attempted to escape from in the first place.

Our vision of what we truly want can only be clear and beneficial once our motivation is no longer based on fear but on our love and enthusiasm for our desire.

When we are free of fear and craving we automatically desire the things we truly love and enjoy.

In the example of the big business desire, once the person has clarity about his or her motivation and is free from fear of lack and survival, one person may still desire running a big business whereas another person may discover his or her true desire as being something completely different and in fact it may have nothing to do with wealth creation at all. A person without fear and craving always attracts wealth.

Awareness of our true motivation for our desire is also required when our motivations have positive conditions. For example let us assume we desire to have a cozy home in order to feel safe and happy. As long as we justify our desire by our need to be secure, our manifestation is flawed. We must be aware of what drives our desire. We should focus our awareness on our need to be safe and happy as a need in its own right, as well as on our desire to own a cozy home. Once we feel happy and safe we move on to manifesting the cozy home. We have to start from where we are and acknowledge our current situation in order to harvest the positive energy that we need to visualize our desired reality. Our subconscious will only hamper the effectiveness of our visualization if there are still negative feelings in us upon which we base our desire.

Another multiple pronged desire to avoid is the following example.

> Instead of visualizing that we have $100,000.00 in order to provide for our child's college education, it is more effective to visualize one of the two things; either that our child's college education is paid for or simply that we have $100,00.00. Which option we chose depends on what we want more. Do we want the $100,00.00 so our child can go to college or do we really want the $100.00.00 and we justify this desire by thinking it is for our child ?

It is fine to combine both desires as long as they are not conditions to each other. The reason is that any condition we attach to our desire is a mental concept. Mental concepts weaken our ability to feel the desired reality as a present moment reality. Mental concepts cannot be experienced. When we use concepts in conjunction with our vision, we engage our minds. Engaging our minds in our visualization process reduces its effectiveness. Our minds are limited by our own patterns, experiences and by our personal history. Hence they limit our power to manifest. In this example if the essence of our desire is that our child can go to college and apart from this desire we do not have a strong desire for money, it may be more effective to visualize that our child is in college and everything is paid for. This way we focus our awareness on what we truly want and leave out anything that would distract us from feeling the reality of our desire as a present moment experience.

The Wealth Formula

When we are grateful we are free from desire. In freedom wealth can be created.

To manifest wealth we must have wealth consciousness. In the absence of poverty consciousness we will have wealth consciousness.

Why do we need to feel wealthy in order become wealthy ?

The answer is that when we know what wealth feels like we will be able to recognize it in the outside world.

When we have wealth consciousness, we manifest wealth because of our love for wealth and not out of a feeling of scarcity. Wanting emphasizes scarcity whereas love fosters abundance.

First we must deconstruct all the things that hold us in a state of poverty consciousness. As a second step we will focus on manifesting wealth.

When we have been freed from poverty consciousness, our inherent positive attitude towards wealth arises. When our fear of survival has disappeared, we begin to feel financially secure. With the help of gratitude we develop lasting wealth consciousness.

However how can we feel grateful if your financial situation is dire ?

The first step is to be non-resistant to whatever situation we are in and not judge our feelings about it. In non-resistance there is nothing for our fear to attach to, so it will dissipate. In the state of non-resistance and acceptance we are able to perceive the positive aspects of our situation and we can be grateful about them. This is not a mental exercise. Rather we use our initial intent to be open and to be able to perceive a positive view about our situation. If we remain non-resistant long enough, eventually our mental activity will subside. At that stage our perception will widen and we will gain intuitive insights about our situation that will help us to see the positive side of our current situation. Being able to perceive positive sides to a situation causes us to be able to see more opportunities. For that we can be grateful for. Our gratitude is the seed for our wealth consciousness.

Our expanded perception will allow for a new consciousness to unfold. This consciousness will be based on a realistic optimism. This new consciousness will be in tune with the financial opportunities that are hidden in our situation. Gratitude transforms hopelessness into empowerment.

Once we are free from our desire for wealth, we are able to experience it to the fullest. By practicing gratitude we become familiar with the feeling of being content and of being free from desire. This is what true wealth feels like.

When all our financial desires have been fulfilled, there is no more desire in us. This is when we experience true wealth.

External wealth is relative. It exists in relation to its environment. Depending on who we compare ourselves with, we feel wealthy or not.

External wealth is temporary. It is prone to change. Internal wealth is permanent. When we are free from our desire for wealth, we feel wealthy. This does not mean that we should not have any desire for financial wealth. However in order to manifest external financial wealth we must experience the state of consciousness of no desire, which is the basis of wealth consciousness.

To illustrate this principle imagine you are in a difficult financial situation. You have a job that you like very much and that provides for the minimum to survive. If you express gratitude for having this job, you become familiar with the feeling of wealth. You do not need to ignore or sugar paint your situation. Gratitude empowers you to expand your perception and it guides your perception into the right direction where the wealth opportunities are. With gratitude we are tapping into the power of eour already existing wealth consciousness. When we become aware of our wealth consciousness we acknowledge its existence and as such allow it to grow. Gratitude is contagious and it spreads. Once we develop a taste for it, we find more and more reasons to be grateful for. Hence we feel more and more content, which in turn fosters wealth creation.

Why is it not enough to understand wealth intellectually ?

The answer is that our mind is limited. It's perception is limited and cannot recognize wealth in all its different forms. With our mind we cannot recognize most of our wealth opportunities. With our mind we will only perceive wealth to the extend to which our individual patterns and experiences allow us.

The reason why some people have poverty consciousness while others appear to be born with wealth consciousness stems from our different individual history and experiences. Intense negative or positive experiences will leave marks in our subconscious. These marks are subconscious memories which create mental patterns. These patterns influence our perceptions and our ability to feel, think and act.

For example a person who has experienced poverty in childhood and is now wealthy may remain to be stuck in poverty consciousness. While another person who experienced financial success early in life may have the perception that he or she can always make money no matter what the circumstances are. We need to be free from the influences of our subconscious patterns. When we are aware of them we become free from them.

By becoming aware of our poverty patterns we detach from them. We will begin to shift these patterns and perceptions to serve us in manifesting wealth.

Jumping from poverty consciousness into manifesting wealth is too fast as it would not enable us to crate a clear and convincing vision of wealth. We would not believe that it is possible for us to be wealthy. Therefore I recommend to manifest in stages.

When we manifest in stages we must be aware of our mind set of scarcity and not resist it. When our fear has diminished we can visualize that we have financial security. This will reinforce our positive outlook. When we add gratitude, we unleash the creative force of love. At that stage we begin to focus on being wealthy. At this point we can have a realistic vision of wealth that we can believe in. This will prevent our subconscious from sabotaging our efforts.

Wealth consciousness not only enables us to effectively manifest wealth but it also ensures that when can receive wealth once it comes to us. Therefore before we visualize wealth we need to be aware of the state we are in at the present moment.

The Power of Surrender

With the help of non-resistance we become detached from our reaction to our circumstances. When we are detached we are able to manifest positive change. As long as we ignore and fight our feelings about the circumstance we are in, we accomplish nothing.

If we cannot let go of our desire for change remain stuck in poverty consciousness. Therefore must completely accept whatever we feel.

The circumstance we want to escape from may contains hidden opportunities. When we surrender we will discover such opportunities.

When I wrote this chapter I had an insightful experience about the power of surrender. One day I was meditating in the temple with my eyes open. A man was standing in front of me blocking my view. I felt annoyed and distracted. Usually what I would do is visualize the person walking away. This time I felt the urge to surrender to the situation. I accepted the opposite of what I desired. Then deep inner peace emerged in me. My eyes closed by themselves and I was dwelling in deep inner peace. Now I was grateful for the man standing in front of me because of him I surrendered and was able to experience this peace. When I finally opened my eyes, the man was gone.

I realized that even though I had given up my desire for the man to walk away, my desire was ultimately fulfilled. I realized that my perception of the annoying situation caused me to completely surrender. Hence my annoyance with the man standing in front of me contained the opportunity to surrender and attain peace. Then when I reached peace there was no more purpose for the man standing there and he disappeared. What I initially desired (for the man to go away) happened just at the right moment.

There are valuable lessons and opportunities hidden in difficult situations. Instead of being too quick to use our intention and visualization to manifest, it is wiser to surrender to the current situation to see if there are hidden opportunities in our current situation. This does not mean that we have to be passive. It simply requires us to be non-resistant to our reaction to our situation. We do not have to give up our desire in order to surrender to our current situation. In the state of non-resistance we keep the door open for the opportunities to reveal themselves. These opportunities may be more than what we could wish for.

In order for our visualizations to work we have to let go of our desire, after we have formed the intent to manifest it.

In my experience, when I opened my eyes and the man was gone I felt freed from my desire. I had already given up on my desire before I opened my eyes. When my desire actually manifested I was able to enjoy it without being attached to it.

When we manifest wealth we use visualization as the active component and surrender (as the passive component of the exercise. After we visualize being wealthy we must let go of our vision and trust that we will receive what is best for us.

Manifesting Traps

Unless we grow our consciousness along with our manifesting powers we will suffer unexpected consequences.

Let me tell you about one of my experiences. One day I visualized that I would receive $1500.00 to pay for a meditation course I wanted to attend. I visualized this money would come from one of my business partners. At that time the business partner regularly sent me small amounts of money as part of a business deal. The amounts of the monthly payments fluctuated based on revenue but were always in the hundreds of dollars and never more than $1000.00 To my surprise this time I received $1600 just in time to pay for the meditation course. Never before had I received this large amount from this business partner. I was ecstatic. My visualization had worked.

The next day however I realized that most of the $1500.00 was reimbursement for my own expenses. It was not profit that I could use for the meditation course.

I realized that there was a lesson to be learned. I had to be more precise with my vision. I should have included that I will receive $1500 that I could spend freely. I should have focused not only on the vision of receiving the particular amount of money but also that I will be happy and able to enjoy this money long term. This might have avoided my subsequent disappointment.

On another occasion I visualized that I would receive $2500 from the same business partner. I challenged myself this time. $2500 would be by far the highest amount I would have ever received from this person and there was no logical reason for this to happen. To my disappointment when the payment came, it was much less than the envisioned $2500.00. I asked my consciousness to teach me the lesson. A sudden insight came to me. Despite the requests of my business partner to send her my invoices on time I had not done so. I felt a rush of energy flowing through my body. I went to my computer and totaled my invoices for the month. After adding them to the money I had received, the total for the month was exactly $2500.00. I was in awe. I realized that if I wanted to be more successful in manifesting I would have to grow my awareness and consciousness. Instead of just visualizing I should have realized that had I sent out my invoices on time, the business partner would have included them in her payment to me for that month and as a matter of common sense this would have increased the chances to receive the desired $2500.00. Had I been more aware I would have acted in sync with my own manifestation and done my part to realize it.

My lesson is that we do not manifest in a vacuum. Our actions, our relationships and our consciousness all have to be in tune for the manifestation to become reality. It is important to develop our awareness and consciousness along with our manifesting powers. Our awareness and consciousness are needed for us to bring about what we truly want and what is best for us. They will avoid that we suffer from pitfalls and unforeseen negative consequences.

We must include in our vision that we are fully surrendering our desire and that we trust our higher consciousness to give us what is truly best for us. By doing so we empower our consciousness to play an active role in our manifestation. The more we focus on our consciousness the more it will grow and support us in manifesting.

Our initial intent is the manifesting force. Our vision is the vehicle for the intent to reach our consciousness.

The traps and pitfalls we encounter bear valuable lessons. When we learn the lessons, our consciousness grows making us better manifesters.

The Hidden Lessons

The more we manifest the more lessons we learn. Often lessons are perceived as negative. However they are important for our progress. In the state of non-resistance we will understand the lesson and learn from it. Sooner or later we receive an insight that relates to our particular circumstance. Sometimes simply by receiving the lesson our perceived negative circumstance disappears and at other times the lesson is an opportunity to grow.

By asking our higher consciousness to teach us the lesson, we acknowledge that our mind cannot figure out the problem on its own. Acknowledging this, empowers our consciousness to deliver the lesson. As long as we attempt to figure out the lesson with our mind we run in circles. By asking to learn the lesson we free our perception from its limitations. Then we can perceive the particular circumstance from a different angle and recognize its positive meaning for us.

In my manifestation practice whenever something happens that I cannot make sense of with my mind, I ask my higher consciousness to show me the lesson. It has worked for me very well.

Whenever we suffer from our circumstances, we should stay with the suffering and ask "to learn the lesson". We must focus on our emotional reaction to the difficult circumstance and not focus on the circumstance itself. The lesson is not hidden in the circumstance but in our feeling and our perception about it. Therefore we must direct our awareness onto our reaction. The external circumstance is neutral. It is neither good nor bad. The lesson is inside of us. It is inside our emotional reaction to the external circumstance.

Manifesting vs.
Materializing

The art of manifesting is based on the principal that all things, circumstances and states are already in existence. By manifesting them, the desired aspect of our consciousness expresses itself on the level of form, where we can experience it. This principal is obvious in regards to internal realities. Any feeling we manifest is already in us and is simply being uncovered and freed from the grip of our mind.

External realities are in existence as well before we manifest them, they just have not yet entered our lives. For example if we desire a particular person to be nicer to us this reality is already dormant in that person and is being activated by the creative forces we initiate in the relationship.

For example when we desire to receive wealth, the wealth is already there in the world. We simply are making ourselves receptive for the wealth to come our way. We are not creating a new reality out of nothing. We are not materializing objects or relationships that were not already in existence. What we do is, we use our consciousness to connect us with the reality we visualize. For example when we visualize to be wealthy, we are making ourselves receptive to receive wealth that is already in existence somewhere in this world.

With our intent we organize and direct the forces to connect us with people and circumstances who will put the wealth into our hands. The person who understands how manifesting works realizes that there is no magic in it.

Manifesting for Others

Manifesting for other people is not only a great virtue but it also is a powerful way to accelerate our manifestation powers.

When we manifest for other people, we have no personal desire and our mind can be detached from the outcome. This does not mean we don't care for the other person. However fact is that we are less influenced by our sub consciousness mind which tends to focus on the non-existence of what we want to manifest.

For example if we visualize that our friend is wealthy there is less mental resistance in us than if we visualize ourselves to be wealthy. When visualizing for others, we are less attached to our own patterns and thoughts which are associated with wealth. Our own poverty consciousness will not affect our vision in the same way. Our patterns are not the same patterns as those of our friend and our subconscious knows this. Our mind may still interfere and make us believe that, for example, our friend can never be wealthy. However since there is less or no emotional charge behind these kinds of subconscious thoughts, they are not as big of an obstacle as they are when we manifest for ourselves.

By practicing for others, we hone our manifestation skills. We can also better observe the process of our manifesting practice and learn from it.

The creative force we use when we manifest for others is compassion. Compassion is very powerful as it is love in its expanded and unconditional form.

When our manifestations for others become reality we receive a tremendous amount of compassion and wisdom in return. This empowers us to grow our consciousness.

What we receive in return is far greater than what we could achieve on our own. The people we direct our compassion at reflect that compassion back at us many times more powerful than what we have given. When we offer compassion, we release the compassion in other people. Compassion gravitates towards itself. When we offer compassion we experience our own compassion as it is reflected back to us.

When we feel compassion, we naturally act unconditionally. Love and compassion are inherently expansive.

When we are loving and compassionate other people will feel it. People gravitate towards people who radiate unconditional love. People want to give to people who radiate love.

Love does not have to be created or acquired. Everything we feel has love in its core. Even our fears and our negative emotions are comprised of love. They are love that has not yet been enlightened by our awareness and consciousness.

When we free ourselves from our fears, anxieties, and cravings, we become receptive to our inherent resources. We begin to love ourselves. We radiate this state of consciousness and we will attract beneficial circumstances and people. We create a virtuous circle of giving and receiving. Since love multiplies when it is reflected, we begin to receive more than we give.

Manifesting Wealth Exercise I Deconstruction

The goal of this exercise is to deconstruct that what keeps us from being wealthy.

Start with the three minute breathing mediation followed by 4 minutes of deep relaxation.

Seven minute Breathing Exercise
Lay down or sit comfortably.

Close your eyes or leave them half way open whatever feels more comfortable.

Become aware of your breath. Do not actively focus on your breath. Be aware that there is breathing inside of you.

Breathe passively. Let the breathing happen and feel the air flowing through your body. Feel your body how it is being touched by your breathing.

Allow your breath to become subtle.

Now become aware of yourself observing your breath. Be aware of your awareness.

Relax and sink deeper. Relax deeper and deeper.

◆ ◆ ◆

Deep Relaxation Exercise for five minutes
For 5 minutes do the deep relaxation exercise.

Relax your body.
Be aware of your body.

Shift your awareness to your feet.
Relax your feet.

Shift your awareness to your lower legs.
Relax your lower legs.

Shift your awareness to your upper legs.
Relax your upper legs.

Shift your awareness to your hips.
Relax your hips.

Shift your awareness to your lower back.
Relax your lower back.

Shift your awareness to your back
Relax your back.

Shift your awareness to your shoulders.
Relax your shoulders.

Michael Rinne

Shift your awareness to your neck.
Relax your neck.

Shift your awareness to your upper arm.
Relax your upper arm.

Shift your awareness to your lower arm.
Relax your lower arm.

Shift your awareness to your hands.
Relax your hands.

Shift your awareness to your belly.
Relax your belly.

Shift your awareness to your chest.
Relax your chest.

Shift your awareness to your throat.
Relax your throat.

Shift your awareness to your lips
Relax your lips.

Shift your awareness to your nose.
Relax your nose.

Shift your awareness to your eyes.
Relax your eyes.

Shift your awareness to your skull.
Relax your skull.

Shift your awareness to the top of your head.
Relax the top of your head.

Inhale deeply.
Hold your breath for 30 seconds then exhale and relax your entire body.

Again inhale deeply.
Hold your breath for 30 seconds then exhale and relax your entire body.

Feel your entire body relaxed.

Feel gratitude for being relaxed. Enjoy the feeling of relaxation and the feeling of gratitude.

Sink deeper and deeper.

If you are sleepy that is fine. You can take a nap.

If you feel you cannot relax do not force it. Accept that you cannot relax. And if you cannot accept that you cannot relax do not worry simply accept whatever is happening inside of you.

Be non-resistant to whatever you feel.

Do not expect any particular result from this exercise.

Sink deeper and enjoy your state. Nobody is judging you.

Relax deeper.

◆ ◆ ◆

Now focus on the feelings you have about wealth.

Focus on why you do not have wealth. If you are already wealthy, focus on why you do not enjoy your wealth to its fullest.

Once you located the feeling of not having wealth, which my be a feeling of scarcity, insecurity, anxiety, wanting, hopelessness etc. let this feeling develop. Be aware of it. Do not push it away or enhance it just let it be as it is.

It may take some time to locate this feeling as you may be used to it to such as degree that it does not stand out. In that case pick a circumstance that you experience often. For example: you are anxious about paying your bills.

When the situation is clearly in front of, you focus on the feeling it triggers in your body.

Once you feel the feeling fully, be non-resistant and express gratitude that you located the feeling.

Your negative feeling about your wealth may linger, or it may grow very strong. Whatever happens let it happen.

If you do not feel anything, simply be aware of how it feels to not feel anything. Do not have any expectation to feel something.

The feeling of scarcity will eventually move and dissipate or it will morph into a different feeling.

Become aware of the new open space in your body and of the new feeling or if there is no new feeling of the emptiness inside of you.

Feel grateful until you fully and intensely feel your gratitude in the form of love. Feel how the love expands throughout your body and beyond its boundaries.

Conclude the exercise.

Manifesting Wealth Exercise II Changing your Perception of Wealth

The goal of this exercise is to change your perception in order to be ready to receive the wealth we desire.

Seven minute Breathing Exercise
Lay down or sit comfortably.

Close your eyes or leave them half way open whatever feels more comfortable.

Become aware of your breath. Do not actively focus on your breath. Be aware that there is breathing inside of you.

Breathe passively. Let the breathing happen and feel the air flowing through your body. Feel your body how it is being touched by your breathing.

Allow your breath to become subtle.

Now become aware of yourself observing your breath. Be aware of your awareness.

Relax and sink deeper. Relax deeper and deeper.

♦ ♦ ♦

Deep Relaxation Exercise for five minutes
For 5 minutes do the deep relaxation exercise.

Relax your body.
Be aware of your body.

Shift your awareness to your feet.
Relax your feet.

Shift your awareness to your lower legs.
Relax your lower legs.

Shift your awareness to your upper legs.
Relax your upper legs.

Shift your awareness to your hips.
Relax your hips.

Shift your awareness to your lower back.
Relax your lower back.

Shift your awareness to your back.
Relax your back.

Shift your awareness to your shoulders.
Relax your shoulders.

Shift your awareness to your neck.
Relax your neck.

Shift your awareness to your upper arm.
Relax your upper arm.

Shift your awareness to your lower arm.
Relax your lower arm.

Shift your awareness to your hands.
Relax your hands.

Shift your awareness to your belly.
Relax your belly.

Shift your awareness to your chest.
Relax your chest.

Shift your awareness to your throat.
Relax your throat.

Shift your awareness to your lips
Relax your lips.

Shift your awareness to your nose.
Relax your nose.

Shift your awareness to your eyes
Relax your eyes.

Shift your awareness to your skull.
Relax your skull.

Shift your awareness to the top of your head.
Relax the top of your head.

Inhale deeply.
Hold your breath for 30 seconds then exhale and relax your entire body.

Again inhale deeply.
Hold your breath for 30 seconds then exhale and relax your entire body.

Feel your entire body relaxed.

Feel gratitude for being relaxed. Enjoy the feeling of relaxation and the feeling of gratitude.

Sink deeper and deeper.

If you are sleepy that is fine. You can take a nap.

If you feel you cannot relax do not force it. Accept that you cannot relax. And if you cannot accept that you cannot relax, do not worry, simply accept whatever is happening inside of you.

Be non-resistant to whatever you feel.

Do not expect any particular result from this exercise.

Sink deeper and enjoy your state. Nobody is judging you.

Relax deeper.

* * *

Now focus on the feeling that is triggered when you think about your wealth or its non-existence in your life.

When you have located the feeling, allow it to develop. Focus your awareness onto the feeling.

It may take some time to locate the feeling.

Once you are aware of your feeling, be non-resistant and express gratitude. Express gratitude and feel how your gratitude emanates love that expands in your body.

Now focus on your perception of your financial situation. Be aware that you are perceiving the situation through your own lenses. Your perception is dependent on your way of seeing things.

Feel how your particular perception is determining your feeling about your wealth. Accept your perception. Be non-resistant to it. There is nothing you can change about your perception. Let it be as it is. Do not judge yourself for having this perception.

Feel how your perception becomes less rigid. A feeling of detachment may arise. Embrace this feeling. Be grateful for this feeling. Express gratitude until you fully and intensely feel the gratitude in your body.

Be aware and see if a new perception of your wealth situation emerges. Do not expect any shift in your perception. Sooner or later this shift will happen. The shift may happen when you least expect it.

This new perception may alter your view about your situation and it may give you the ability to perceive more beneficial angles of your situation. It may also help you change your financial situation as well.

Conclude the exercise.

Manifesting Wealth
Exercise III
Visualizing Wealth

The goal of this exercise is to create a clear and realistic image of being wealthy and to experience yourself as being in the present moment.

If you feel you are not ready to create a vision of wealth because you are still occupied with your fear of scarcity or you feel unable to have a clear perception of wealth, feel free to do the previous two exercises again on day 21 before you do this exercise.

Seven minute Breathing Exercise
Lay down or sit comfortably.

Close your eyes or leave them half way open whatever feels more comfortable.

Become aware of your breath. Do not actively focus on your breath. Be aware that there is breathing inside of you.

Breathe passively. Let the breathing happen and feel the air flowing through your body. Feel your body how it is being touched by your breathing.

Allow your breath to become subtle.

Now become aware of yourself observing your breath. Be aware of your awareness.

Relax and sink deeper. Relax deeper and deeper.

♦ ♦ ♦

Deep Relaxation Exercise for five minutes
For 5 minutes do the deep relaxation exercise.

Relax your body.
Be aware of your body.

Shift your awareness to your feet.
Relax your feet.

Shift your awareness to your lower legs.
Relax your lower legs.

Shift your awareness to your upper legs.
Relax your upper legs.

Shift your awareness to your hips.
Relax your hips.

Shift your awareness to your lower back.
Relax your lower back.

Shift your awareness to your back.
Relax your back.

Shift your awareness to your shoulders.
Relax your shoulders.

Shift your awareness to your neck.
Relax your neck.

Shift your awareness to your upper arm.
Relax your upper arm.

Shift your awareness to your lower arm.
Relax your lower arm.

Shift your awareness to your hands.
Relax your hands.

Shift your awareness to your belly.
Relax your belly.

Shift your awareness to your chest.
Relax your chest.

Shift your awareness to your throat.
Relax your throat.

Shift your awareness to your lips..Relax your upper arm.

Shift your awareness to your lower arm.
Relax your lower arm.

Shift your awareness to your hands.
Relax your hands.

Shift your awareness to your belly.
Relax your belly.

Shift your awareness to your chest.
Relax your chest.

Shift your awareness to your throat.
Relax your throat.

Shift your awareness to your lips
Relax your lips.

Shift your awareness to your nose.
Relax your nose.

Shift your awareness to your eyes
Relax your eyes.

Shift your awareness to your skull.
Relax your skull.

Shift your awareness to the top of your head.
Relax the top of your head.

Inhale deeply.
Hold your breath for 30 seconds then exhale and relax your entire body.

Again inhale deeply.
Hold your breath for 30 seconds then exhale and relax your entire body.

Feel your entire body relaxed.

Feel gratitude for being relaxed. Enjoy the feeling of relaxation and the feeling of gratitude.

Sink deeper and deeper.

If you are sleepy that is fine. You can take a nap.

If you feel you cannot relax do not force it. Accept that you cannot relax. And if you cannot accept that you cannot relax do not worry simply accept whatever is happening inside of you.

Be non-resistant to whatever you feel.

Do not expect any particular result from this exercise.

Sink deeper and enjoy your state. Nobody is judging you.

Relax deeper.

◆ ◆ ◆

Now be aware of how you feel right now. Be non-resistant to whatever you feel.

Once you are relaxed, begin to create your vision of yourself being wealthy.

If you cannot think of how to create the vision you can write down how you want to feel being wealthy, how much money you want to have and what objects you want to have.

Do not create any feeling. Be open and non-resistant. Feelings of joy and wealth will arise when you observe yourself in the vision.

Do not hold on to any feeling.

Now express gratitude that you are able to have this vision and that you feel wealthy. Feel your gratitude.

Be aware of how your gratitude feeds your vision with positive creative energy.

When you have reached the point where you have a present moment experience about your vision and your feelings about it are intensely felt as happening in the present moment, let go of your vision.

Surrender everything you have created in the vision and be non-resistant. If you cannot let go and continue to create the vision be non-resistant to that as well.

Trust that your higher consciousness will provide you with whatever you desire in its best possible form.

Conclude the exercise.

Achieving Permanent Transformation

In life, we mostly act and react the same way over and over again. We think the same thoughts and we feel the same emotions because we have the same mind with its same old subconscious patterns.

Does anything ever change ?

The answer is yes. We can brake through this repetitive cycle when we change our subconscious patterns. With the practice of awareness, our feelings will change. The people's reactions to our actions will change as well. Our actions and reactions cause us to have new experiences.

This is how we start a virtuous cycle of new experiences that will form new positive patterns in us. The new patterns replace the old patterns. Our subconscious changes due to our new patters. Thus we become permanently transformed.

For example whereas in the past, a person may have triggered a defensive pattern in us, now this same person may trigger compassion in us. This is due to our transformed patterns, causing new reactions. Once we have gained new positive experiences their effect on our old patterns will be that the patterns lose their emotional charge. Now whenever we encounter this particular person, we feel compassion, which is the default reaction to any circumstance, in the absence of any other pattern.

Patterns are being formed by intense experiences throughout our lifetime. They influence our feelings and emotions and make us react in a certain way. With the help of awareness we will replace all negative patterns with positive patterns and with no patterns at all.

When we have no more negative patterns we will no longer suffer under our circumstances. When the most illusive of all patterns; our Self is de-charged and we become detached from it, we experience ultimate freedom.

When there are no more patterns in us, our default reaction to any circumstance will be compassion.

At first this transformation is not permanent. We will go back and forth between our old patterns and our new states. The more intense our experiences become, the more permanently we become transformed. At that stage we will no longer need to visualize in order for our desires to manifest. We will manifest with our intent alone.

When we are permanently transformed we are able to permanently enjoy our manifestations.

We can rest assured that we are already beginning to be permanently transformed in many areas of our life at this very moment.

Life Beyond Manifesting

Our manifestation skills will evolve throughout our practice. In the beginning it is a technique comprised of visualizing and getting ourselves in tune with the desire. The more we progress, we will realize that we can manifest with our mere intent.

Eventually a shift in us will happen, which will lead to our detachment from all form. Our cravings for certain things and feelings will disappear and we begin to dwell more and more in our essence. The more we dwell in our essence, detached from duality, the more our desires disappear. At that stage all we will do is simply act.

Our actions become unconditional. Our actions will always have a positive effect on us. There will be no reactions, only actions and our actions appear to be automatic and guided by our consciousness.

More and more we will become the source from which everything expands and to which everything gravitates. We will experience our essence through its reflection in other people. We will move closer and closer to the core of our essence. In its core there is no experience and no knowing, there is only beingness.

Whatever we desire, we will receive. We will dwell in our physical form and enjoy everything we experience. We will no longer need our intent to manifest either. Our way of life, our actions and our state of being will naturally provide for us and we will enjoy it without attachment.

There is no need to give up on manifesting. We do not need to only focus on reaching the state of absolute essence. Our practice will naturally guide us there. Once our awareness and consciousness are developed, they will enlighten all corners of our Self and lead us to the highest state when the time is ripe.

What to do Next

Nothing in this book shall be viewed as a teaching. If the book inspires you to venture out and find your own path and to make your own experiences, then the purpose of this book has been fulfilled.

The exercises in this book are based on a 21 day Manifesting program. It is recommended to purchase the audio book which includes the 21 guided exercises along with this book.

In the 21 day online program you will be able to listen to the guided exercises.

I encourage you to venture out to find your own path to a more happy, successful and wealthy life. Please send me an email to start a dialog about your own experiences and to ask questions.

Go to my Facebook Page at https://www.facebook.com/tensuccess-formulas/ to find out about upcoming seminars, books, and other help and to connect with other like minded people.

Love

Michael Rinne

www.ingramcontent.com/pod-product-compliance
Lightning Source LLC
Chambersburg PA
CBHW072341090426
42741CB00012B/2870